The Lost Pearl of Yushan
渔山遗珠

The Boutique Atlas of "Xiaobaijiao Ⅰ"
Shipwreck in Xiangshan of Ningbo

宁波象山"小白礁Ⅰ号"
出水文物精品图录

编著　宁波市文物考古研究所
　　　象山县文物管理委员会办公室
　　　国家文物局水下文化遗产保护中心

宁波出版社

编辑委员会

主　　　任　赵惠峰　柴晓明
副 主 任　舒月明　徐建成　王结华　孙　键
主　　　编　王结华
执行主编　林国聪
副 主 编　王光远　金　涛　郑松才
编　　务　罗　鹏　许　超　雷　少　贺俊彦
　　　　　　　史　伟　梅术文
摄　　影　冯　毅　孙　臣　李朱佳　代威巍
翻　　译　周昳恒　洪　欣

Compilation Institues

Ningbo Municipal Institute of Cultural Relics and Archaeology
Cultural Heritage Management Commission Office of Xiangshan County
National Center of Underwater Cultural Heritage

Editorial Committee

Directors：Zhao Huifeng　Chai Xiaoming
Deputy Directors：Shu Yueming　Xu Jiancheng　Wang Jiehua　Sun Jian
Chief Editor：Wang Jiehua
Executive Chief Editor：Lin Guocong
Associate Chief Editors：Wang Guangyuan　Jin Tao　Zheng Songcai
Editors：Luo Peng　Xu Chao　Lei Shao　He Junye　Shi Wei　Mei Shuwen
Photographers：Feng Yi　Sun Chen　Li Zhujia　Dai Weiwei
Translators：Zhou Yiheng　Hong Xin

目 录

概述 ·· 01

篇章一 青花瓷

1 嘉庆款青花缠枝花卉纹碗（2014NXXBW1:38）·· 18
2 嘉庆款青花缠枝花卉纹碗（2012NXXBW1:122）·· 20
3 嘉庆款青花缠枝花卉纹碗（2014NXXBW1:10）·· 22
4 道光款青花缠枝花卉纹碗（2012NXXBW1:42）·· 24
5 道光款青花缠枝花卉纹碗（2012NXXBW1:43）·· 26
6 嘉庆款青花缠枝花卉纹碗（2012NXXBW1:120）·· 28
7 嘉庆款青花缠枝花卉纹碗（2014NXXBW1:62）·· 30
8 道光款青花缠枝花卉纹碗（2012NXXBW1:21）·· 32
9 道光款青花缠枝花卉纹碗（2012NXXBW1:24）·· 34
10 道光款青花缠枝花卉纹碗（2014NXXBW1:18）·· 36
11 青花缠枝花卉纹碗（2009NXXBW1:116）·· 38
12 青花草叶纹碗（2014NXXBW1:57）·· 44
13 青花花草纹碗（2009NXXBW1:4）··· 46
14 青花花草纹碗（2009NXXBW1:5）··· 48
15 青花花草纹碗（2014NXXBW1:2）··· 50
16 青花竖线纹碗（2014NXXBW1:116）·· 52
17 青花折线纹碗（2014NXXBW1:78）··· 53
18 青花灵芝纹碗（2014NXXBW1:61）··· 54
19 青花灵芝纹碗（2014NXXBW1:63）··· 56
20 青花花草纹菱口豆（2014NXXBW1:40）··· 58

21	青花花草纹菱口豆（2014NXXBW1:64）	60
22	青花花草纹菱口豆（2012NXXBW1:71）	62
23	青花花草纹菱口豆（2014NXXBW1:15）	64
24	青花花草纹菱口豆（2014NXXBW1:55）	66
25	青花花草纹菱口豆（2014NXXBW1:41）	68
26	青花花草纹菱口豆（2014NXXBW1:42）	70
27	青花灵芝纹盘（2012NXXBW1:81）	74
28	青花菊瓣纹"福"款盘（2012NXXBW1:78）	76
29	青花菊瓣纹"福"款盘（2012NXXBW1:79）	77
30	青花草叶纹盘（2008NXXBW1:4）	78
31	青花缠枝花卉纹杯（2009NXXBW1:81）	80
32	青花缠枝花卉纹杯（2014NXXBW1:138）	82
33	青花缠枝花卉纹碟（2014NXXBW1:119）	83
34	青花缠枝花草纹灯盏（2008NXXBW1:16）	84
35	青花缠枝花卉纹盖（2009NXXBW1:12）	86
36	青花缠枝花草纹勺（2014NXXBW1:7）	88
37	青花缠枝花草纹勺（2014NXXBW1:101）	89

篇章二　五彩瓷

1	五彩碗（2012NXXBW1:82）	92
2	五彩碗（2012NXXBW1:83）	93
3	五彩盖罐（盖，2009NXXBW1:16；罐，2009NXXBW1:27）	94
4	五彩盖罐（盖，2009NXXBW1:474；罐，2009NXXBW1:475）	96
5	五彩盖罐（盖，2009NXXBW1:25；罐，2014NXXBW1:449）	98
6	五彩器盖（2012NXXBW1:88）	100
7	五彩器盖（2009NXXBW1:20）	101
8	五彩器盖（2009NXXBW1:23）	102
9	五彩器盖（2014NXXBW1:100）	103
10	五彩器盖（2012NXXBW1:86）	104

篇章三 陶器

1　紫砂壶（2012NXXBW1:91）　　108
2　紫砂罐（2014NXXBW1:60）　　110
3　酱釉陶壶（2009NXXBW1:31）　　112
4　酱釉陶壶（2012NXXBW1:90）　　114
5　酱釉陶罐（2008NXXBW1:9）　　115
6　酱釉四系陶罐（2014NXXBW1:30）　　116
7　酱釉陶罐（2014NXXBW1:103）　　117
8　酱釉陶罐（2014NXXBW1:105）　　118
9　酱釉凤穿牡丹花卉纹子口盖（2012NXXBW1:89）　　119

篇章四 金属器

1　测深铅锤（2014NXXBW1:65）　　122
2　银饼（2014NXXBW1:450）　　123
3　西班牙银币（2008NXXBW1:11）　　124
4　康熙通宝（2009NXXBW1:39）　　125
5　雍正通宝（2014NXXBW1:96）　　126
6　乾隆通宝（2009NXXBW1:57）　　127
7　嘉庆通宝（2009NXXBW1:70）　　128
8　道光通宝（2009NXXBW1:76）　　129
9　宽永通宝（2009NXXBW1:78）　　130
10　景兴通宝（2009NXXBW1:77）　　131
11　铜螺栓（2014NXXBW1:3）　　132
12　铜盖（2008NXXBW1:14）　　133
13　陀螺状铜构件（2012NXXBW1:93）　　134

篇章五 其他器物

1　"源合盛记"印章（2008NXXBW1:12）　　138
2　毛笔（2014NXXBW1:68）　　139

3	砚台底座（2014NXXBW1:1）	140
4	石板（2014NXXBW1:371）	141

篇章六　船体构件

1	首龙骨	144
2	主龙骨	145
3	尾龙骨	146
4	肋骨（肋东 5）	148
5	肋骨（肋东 13）	150
6	肋骨（肋东 16）	152
7	肋骨（肋东 21）	154
8	肋骨（肋东 22）	156
9	肋骨（肋西 11）	157
10	隔舱板（隔 1）	158
11	隔舱板（隔 2）	160
12	隔舱板（隔 3）	161
13	船壳内层板（壳东 2-2/5）	162
14	船壳外层板（壳西 3-2/5）	164
15	铺舱板（垫 3）	166
16	铺舱板（垫 16）	168
17	铺舱板（垫 27）	169
18	船壳外层板（壳东 7 下 -3/4）	170
19	顶杠	171
20	桅座	172

后记 ········· 174

CONTENTS

Introduction 01

Chapter I Blue-and-white Porcelain

1 Blue-and-white Bowl with Dated Inscription of Jiaqing Reign and Flower Scrolls
   （2014NXXBW1∶38） 18

2 Blue-and-white Bowl with Dated Inscription of Jiaqing Reign and Flower Scrolls
   （2012NXXBW1∶122） 20

3 Blue-and-white Bowl with Dated Inscription of Jiaqing Reign and Flower Scrolls
   （2014NXXBW1∶10） 22

4 Blue-and-white Bowl with Dated Inscription of Daoguang Reign and Flower Scrolls
   （2012NXXBW1∶42） 24

5 Blue-and-white Bowl with Dated Inscription of Daoguang Reign and Flower Scrolls
   （2012NXXBW1∶43） 26

6 Blue-and-white Bowl with Dated Inscription of Jiaqing Reign and Flower Scrolls
   （2012NXXBW1∶120） 28

7 Blue-and-white Bowl with Dated Inscription of Jiaqing Reign and Flower Scrolls
   （2014NXXBW1∶62） 30

8 Blue-and-white Bowl with Dated Inscription of Daoguang Reign and Flower Scrolls
   （2012NXXBW1∶21） 32

9 Blue-and-white Bowl with Dated Inscription of Daoguang Reign and Flower Scrolls
   （2012NXXBW1∶24） 34

10 Blue-and-white Bowl with Dated Inscription of Daoguang Reign and Flower Scrolls
   （2014NXXBW1∶18） 36

11 Blue-and-white Bowl with Flower Scrolls（2009NXXBW1∶116） 39

12 Blue-and-white Bowl with Leaves Design（2014NXXBW1∶57） 44

13 Blue-and-white Bowl with Floral Design（2009NXXBW1∶4） 46

14 Blue-and-white Bowl with Floral Design（2009NXXBW1∶5） 48

15	Blue-and-white Bowl with Floral Design (2014NXXBW1:2)	50
16	Blue-and-white Bowl with Linear Pattern (2014NXXBW1:116)	52
17	Blue-and-white Bowl with Wave Pattern (2014NXXBW1:78)	53
18	Blue-and-white Bowl with Fungus Design (2014NXXBW1:61)	54
19	Blue-and-white Bowl with Fungus Design (2014NXXBW1:63)	56
20	Blue-and-white Lobed Stem Plate with Floral Design (2014NXXBW1:40)	58
21	Blue-and-white Lobed Stem Plate with Floral Design (2014NXXBW1:64)	60
22	Blue-and-white Lobed Stem Plate with Floral Design (2012NXXBW1:71)	62
23	Blue-and-white Lobed Stem Plate with Floral Design (2014NXXBW1:15)	64
24	Blue-and-white Lobed Stem Plate with Floral Design (2014NXXBW1:55)	66
25	Blue-and-white Lobed Stem Plate with Floral Design (2014NXXBW1:41)	68
26	Blue-and-white Lobed Stem Plate with Floral Design (2014NXXBW1:42)	70
27	Blue-and-white Plate with Fungus Design (2012NXXBW1:81)	74
28	Blue-and-white Plate with Chrysanthemum Petal and *Fu* Inscription (2012NXXBW1:78)	76
29	Blue-and-white Plate with Chrysanthemum Petal and *Fu* Inscription (2012NXXBW1:79)	77
30	Blue-and-white Plate with Leaves Design (2008NXXBW1:4)	78
31	Blue-and-white Cup with Flower Scrolls (2009NXXBW1:81)	80
32	Blue-and-white Cup with Flower Scrolls (2014NXXBW1:138)	82
33	Blue-and-white Dish with Flower Scrolls (2014NXXBW1:119)	83
34	Blue-and-white Lamp with Floral Scrolls (2008NXXBW1:16)	84
35	Blue-and-white Lid with Flower Scrolls (2009NXXBW1:12)	86
36	Blue-and-white Spoon with Floral Scrolls (2014NXXBW1:7)	88
37	Blue-and-white Spoon with Floral Scrolls (2014NXXBW1:101)	89

Chapter II Famille Verte Porcelain

1	Famille Verte Bowl (2012NXXBW1:82)	92
2	Famille Verte Bowl (2012NXXBW1:83)	93
3	Famille Verte Jar (Lid, 2009NXXBW1:16; Jar, 2009NXXBW1:27)	94
4	Famille Verte Jar (Lid, 2009NXXBW1:474; Jar, 2009NXXBW1:475)	96
5	Famille Verte Jar (Lid, 2009NXXBW1:25; Jar, 2014NXXBW1:449)	98

6	Famille Verte Lid（2012NXXBW1∶88）	100
7	Famille Verte Lid（2009NXXBW1∶20）	101
8	Famille Verte Lid（2009NXXBW1∶23）	102
9	Famille Verte Lid（2014NXXBW1∶100）	103
10	Famille Verte Lid（2012NXXBW1∶86）	104

Chapter III Pottery

1	Yixing Clay Teapot（2012NXXBW1∶91）	108
2	Yixing Clay Jar（2014NXXBW1∶60）	110
3	Brown Glazed Ewer（2009NXXBW1∶31）	112
4	Brown Glazed Ewer（2012NXXBW1∶90）	114
5	Brown Glazed Jar（2008NXXBW1∶9）	115
6	Brown Glazed Jar with Four Rings（2014NXXBW1∶30）	116
7	Brown Glazed Jar（2014NXXBW1∶103）	117
8	Brown Glazed Jar（2014NXXBW1∶105）	118
9	Brown Glazed Lid with Phoenix amid Peony Scolls（2012NXXBW1∶89）	119

Chapter IV Metal Artefact

1	Sounding Lead（2014NXXBW1∶65）	122
2	Discoid Silver（2014NXXBW1∶450）	123
3	Spanish Silver Coin（2008NXXBW1∶11）	124
4	Kangxi Tongbao Coin（2009NXXBW1∶39）	125
5	Yongzheng Tongbao Coin（2014NXXBW1∶96）	126
6	Qianlong Tongbao Coin（2009NXXBW1∶57）	127
7	Jiaqing Tongbao Coin（2009NXXBW1∶70）	128
8	Daoguang Tongbao Coin（2009NXXBW1∶76）	129
9	Kan'ei Tongbao Coin（2009NXXBW1∶78）	130
10	King Hing Tongbao Coin（2009NXXBW1∶77）	131
11	Copper Bolt（2014NXXBW1∶3）	132
12	Copper Cover（2008NXXBW1∶14）	133
13	Turbinated Copper Element（2012NXXBW1∶93）	134

Chapter V Other Artefact

1	Seal with *Yuan He Sheng Ji* Inscription (2008NXXBW1:12)	138
2	Calligraphy Painting Brush (2014NXXBW1:68)	139
3	Inkstone Stand (2014NXXBW1:1)	140
4	Stone Slab (2014NXXBW1:371)	141

Chapter VI Ship Structural Component

1	Stem	144
2	Keel	145
3	Stern	146
4	Frame (Eastern Frame No.5)	148
5	Frame (Eastern Frame No.13)	150
6	Frame (Eastern Frame No.16)	152
7	Frame (Eastern Frame No.21)	154
8	Frame (Eastern Frame No.22)	156
9	Frame (Western Frame No.11)	157
10	Bulkhead (Bulkhead No.1)	158
11	Bulkhead (Bulkhead No.2)	160
12	Bulkhead (Bulkhead No.3)	161
13	Shell (Eastern Shell 2-2/5)	162
14	2nd Layer of Shell (Western Shell 3-2/5)	164
15	Dunnage Board (Dunnage Board No.3)	166
16	Dunnage Board (Dunnage Board No.16)	168
17	Dunnage Board (Dunnage Board No.27)	169
18	2nd Layer of Shell (Eastern Shell No.7 Bottom-3/4)	170
19	Propping Rod	171
20	Mast Base	172

Postscript 174

概 述

宁波，古称明州，明初改称宁波，寓意"海定则波宁"。

昔日之明州，曾经是我国"海上丝绸之路"的始发港之一和中国大运河最南端的出海口；今日之宁波，依然是我国对外经贸往来的繁华滨海城市和重要海运港口。

从宁波象山石浦港出发，朝东南方向航行大约26海里，便到达了我国领海线基点之一的渔山列岛。古代时，这里曾是海上贸易与对外交流的咽喉要道；如今，这里已是海钓者的基地和旅行者的天堂。

2008年10月，一支由中国国家博物馆和宁波市文物考古研究所领衔，由来自全国各地的水下考古队员组成的工作队伍在渔山列岛开展浙江沿海水下文物普查，在北渔山岛小白礁畔距海底24米处发现了一艘清代道光年间的木质沉船，这就是后来蜚声中外的"小白礁Ⅰ号"。

2009年6月，根据第三次全国文物普查的工作安排，水下考古工作队再次来到北渔山岛，对"小白礁Ⅰ号"展开重点调查和试掘，基本明确了沉船的分布范围、层位堆积、保存状况和文化内涵等信息。

2011年4月，国家文物局批准同意对"小白礁Ⅰ号"进行发掘，是为宁波市、浙江省首个正式获批的水下考古发掘项目，也是近年来国家水下文化遗产保护的重点项目之一。

2012年6至7月，由国家水下文化遗产保护中心（现国家文物局水下文化遗产保护中心）牵头组织，宁波市文物考古研究所（国家水下文化遗产保护宁波基地）具体实施，来自全国各地的水下考古队员共同组队，基本完成了"小白礁Ⅰ号"船载文物的发掘工作。

2013年4月，国家文物局批复同意"小白礁Ⅰ号"船体现场保护与保护修复（Ⅰ期）项目立项。

2014年5至7月，国家文物局水下文化遗产保护中心与宁波市文物考古研究所（国家水下文化遗产保护宁波基地）再次组队，来自国内外的20多名水下考古队员和多家知名科研院所的30余名技术人员齐聚渔山，出色完成了"小白礁Ⅰ号"船体发掘与现场保护任务。

2014年10月，位于宁波市北仑区春晓滨海新城的国家水下文化遗产保护宁波基地正式建成投用，设于宁波基地内的"水下考古在中国"专题陈列同步对外开放，"小白礁Ⅰ号"水下考古发掘场景与部分船载文物在陈列中惊艳亮相，其船体构件也在宁波基地沉船修复展示室内边保护边展示，使公众共享水下考古与水下文化遗产保护的成果。至此，"小白礁Ⅰ号"水下考古发掘项目圆满落幕。

历时六年之久的水下考古调查与发掘情况显示："小白礁Ⅰ号"为一艘沉没于清代道光年间（1821—1850）的远洋木质商船。船体残长约20.35米，宽约7.85米，出水有龙骨、肋骨、船壳外层板、隔舱板、铺舱板、桅座等船体构件共240余件，造船所用木材主要产自东南亚一带。经初步分析研究，"小白礁Ⅰ号"在船体构造上既具有典型的中国古代造船工艺的特征，也保留了一些国外的造船传统，可以说是中外造船技术相互融合的难得的实物例证。

"小白礁Ⅰ号"共出水船载文物1060余件，主要包括：品相精美的青花瓷碗、豆、盘、杯、碟、灯盏、盖、勺；色彩斑驳的五彩瓷碗、罐、盖；名家制作的紫砂壶；标明商号的玉石印章；木质砚台底座；竹竿朱毫毛笔；大清"康熙通宝"、"雍正通宝"、"乾隆通宝"、"嘉庆通宝"、"道光通宝"、日本"宽永通宝"、越南"景兴通宝"、西班牙银币，以及宁波本地特产的石板材等。这些"重见天日"的珍贵文物是源远流长、生生不息的"海上丝绸之路"在宁波持续辉煌的有力见证，在历史、科学研究中具有重要的学术价值。

"小白礁Ⅰ号"水下考古发掘项目不仅因其众多珍贵的出水文物和"中西合璧"的船体构造为社会所关注，更因其先进的工作理念、科学的考古方法、创新的科技应用、超前的保护意识和多重的安全保障为业界所称道，为国家文物局即将颁布的《水下考古工作规程（试行）》提供了宝贵的实践经验，被誉为"我国水下考古走向水下文化遗产保护的又一重要标识"和"我国水下考古的又一创新之作"。

"小白礁Ⅰ号"水下考古期间，国内外数十家媒体进行了全方位、多角度、跟踪式的宣传报道。特别是2012年发掘时，在国家文物局和浙江省文物局高度重视与大力支持，宁波市委和市政府统筹谋划与指挥协调，象山县委和县政府积极配合与提供保障，各级宣传、文化、广电、财政、通信、电力、交通、海洋、海事、气象等职能部门信息互通与分工协作下，中央电视台、宁波电视台连续多天推出多场"直击'小白礁

Ⅰ号'水下考古"直播特别节目。其时,"小白礁Ⅰ号"水下考古与"神九"飞天、"蛟龙"入海同步直播,同台亮相,为社会各界和广大市民奉献上了一道精彩的文化盛宴,水下考古也成为宣传历史名城与港城宁波的又一张靓丽的文化名片。

"水下考古全国一盘棋。""小白礁Ⅰ号"水下考古项目的成功立项、顺利实施与圆满收官,离不开上上下下的倾力合作,更离不开方方面面的鼎力支持。在此,我们对所有相关单位及个人表示衷心的感谢。

致谢单位:

国家文物局

中国文化遗产研究院

国家文物局水下文化遗产保护中心

中国国家博物馆

浙江省文物局

宁波市委、市政府

宁波市委宣传部

宁波市文化广电新闻出版局

宁波市财政税务局

宁波海事局

宁波市海洋与渔业局

宁波市港航管理局

宁波市广播电视集团

象山县委、县政府

象山县委宣传部

象山县文化广电新闻出版局

宁波海事局象山海事处

象山县海洋与渔业局

象山县公安边防大队

石浦镇政府

石浦边防派出所

渔山村村民委员会

……

致谢个人：

文化部副部长、国家文物局局长	励小捷
文化部党组成员、故宫博物院院长	单霁翔
国家文物局副局长	童明康
国家文物局副局长	顾玉才
国家文物局文物保护与考古司司长	关　强
国家文物局办公室副主任	闫亚林
国家文物局文物保护与考古司考古处处长	张　磊
国家文物局政策法规司新闻与宣传处处长	范伊然
国家文物局人事司专家与培训处处长	佟　薇
国家文物局文物保护与考古司文物处副处长	张　凌
国家文物局文物保护与考古司考古处副处长	王　铮
国家文物局文物保护与考古司考古处副调研员	王　彬
中国文化遗产研究院院长	刘曙光
国家文物局水下文化遗产保护中心主任	柴晓明
国家文物局水下文化遗产保护中心党支部书记	张　威
国家文物局水下文化遗产保护中心副主任	宋建忠
国家文物局水下文化遗产保护中心主任助理	王大民
国家文物局水下文化遗产保护中心水下考古研究所所长	姜　波
国家文物局水下文化遗产保护中心办公室主任	赵嘉斌
国家文物局水下文化遗产保护中心技术总监	孙　键
国家文物局水下文化遗产保护中心技术与装备处副主任	李　滨
浙江省文化厅原巡视员、省文物局原局长	鲍贤伦
浙江省文化厅副厅长、省文物局局长	陈　瑶
浙江省文化厅副巡视员、省文物局副局长	吴志强
浙江省文物局副局长	郑建华
浙江省文物局文物保护与考古处副处长	许常丰
宁波市文化广电新闻出版局原局长	陈佳强
宁波市文化广电新闻出版局局长	赵惠峰
宁波市文化广电新闻出版局副局长	孟建耀

宁波市文化广电新闻出版局副局长	舒月明
宁波市文化广电新闻出版局文物与博物馆处处长	徐建成
象山县文化广电新闻出版局局长	任先顺
象山县文化广电新闻出版局副局长	董　云
象山县文物管理委员会办公室主任	郑松才
"小白礁Ⅰ号"主要线索提供者	牟永根

……

合作单位：

中国文化遗产研究院

中国科学院

北京大学

浙江大学

中山大学

武汉理工大学

交通部广州打捞局

上海劳雷工业有限公司

镇海满洋船务有限公司

武汉海达数云技术有限公司

北京国洋联合潜水运动有限公司

宁波石浦渔山水产养殖有限公司

……

参与队员：

国家文物局水下文化遗产保护中心	赵嘉斌
国家文物局水下文化遗产保护中心	孙　键
国家文物局水下文化遗产保护中心	李　滨
国家文物局水下文化遗产保护中心	周春水
国家文物局水下文化遗产保护中心	邓启江
国家文物局水下文化遗产保护中心	孟原召
国家文物局水下文化遗产保护中心	鄂　杰
国家文物局水下文化遗产保护中心	梁国庆

国家文物局水下文化遗产保护中心	王亦晨
国家文物局水下文化遗产保护中心	赵哲昊
中国国家博物馆	朱砚山
中国国家博物馆	邱秀华
中国国家博物馆水下考古科研与培训基地	陈建国
辽宁省文物考古研究所	冯 雷
烟台市博物馆	孙兆锋
蓬莱市文物管理局	赵 鹏
海军博物馆	王 鹏
南京博物院	王 茜
安徽省文物考古研究所	张 辉
福建博物院	羊泽林
福州市文物考古工作队	朱 滨
福州市文物考古工作队	张 勇
泉州市博物馆	张红兴
漳州市文物保护管理所	阮永好
吉安市博物馆	曾 瑾
广东省文物考古研究所	黎飞艳
海南省博物馆	韩 飞
海南省博物馆	蔡敷隆*
海南省博物馆	黄 康*
德国考古研究院欧亚考古研究所	禾多米
舟山市文物保护考古所	司久玉
舟山市文物保护考古所	任记国
象山县文物管理委员会办公室	贺俊彦
象山县文物管理委员会办公室	史 伟
宁波市文物考古研究所	林国聪
宁波市文物考古研究所	王光远
宁波市文物考古研究所	金 涛

*蔡敷隆、黄康现已辞职转行。

宁波市文物考古研究所	罗 鹏
宁波市文物考古研究所	许 超
宁波市文物考古研究所	雷 少
宁波市文物考古研究所	李泽琛
水下考古设备技师	范开泰
水下考古设备技师	刘春健
水下考古设备技师	甘慰元

……

值此图录出版之际，谨向上述单位和个人再次表示真挚的谢忱！

主要参考资料：

1. 中国国家博物馆水下考古研究中心、宁波市文物考古研究所：《浙江宁波渔山小白礁一号沉船遗址调查与试掘》，载《中国国家博物馆馆刊》2011年第11期。

2. 宁波市文物考古研究所、国家文物局水下文化遗产保护中心：《浙江象山县"小白礁Ⅰ号"清代沉船2012年发掘简报》，载《考古》2015年第6期。

3. 宁波市文物考古研究所、国家文物局水下文化遗产保护中心，林国聪、王结华、姜波执笔：《我国水下考古的又一创新之作——浙江宁波象山"小白礁Ⅰ号"2014年度发掘》，载《中国文物报》2014年8月29日第5版。

4. 林国聪、王结华：《"小白礁Ⅰ号"水下考古项目管理与创新》，载《新技术·新方法·新思路——首届"水下考古·宁波论坛"文集》，科学出版社，2015年10月。

5. 国家文物局水下文化遗产保护中心、宁波市文物考古研究所：《水下24米——浙江宁波象山"小白礁Ⅰ号"水下考古实录》，中国广播电视出版社，2014年6月。

Introduction

Ningbo was once called Mingzhou. The emperor in the early Ming Dynasty changed its name to Ningbo, with a good wish of "peaceful ocean and waves".

The Mingzhou city in the history was once one of the origin ports of the "Maritime Silk Road" and the southernmost estuary of China Grand Canal. Today the flourishing city and maritime port Ningbo still plays a vital role in foreign economy and trade.

Yushan Archipelago as one of the cardinal points of China's territorial sea borderline, is located 26 nautical miles to the southeast of Shipu Port of Xiangshan County of Ningbo. The port was once the key point of the foreign trade and communication, but now becomes a heaven for travellers and a base for sea-fishing.

In October 2008, a team of underwater archaeologists from all over the country led by the National Museum of China and Ningbo Municipal Institute of Cultural Relics and Archaeology conducted an investigation of underwater heritage alongside the coastal line of Zhejiang Province. During the investigation, a wooden shipwreck from Daoguang Reign of Qing Dynasty was discovered in the depth of 24 meters under the sea near Xiaobaijiao Reef of Yushan Archipelago. The shipwreck named as "Xiaobaijiao I" later gains its reputation across the world.

In June 2009, following the plan of the Third National Cultural Heritage General Investigation, the underwater archaeological team conducted a major survey and an exploratory excavation of "Xiaobaijiao I" shipwreck in Yushan Archipelago. This time, the location, taphonomy, preservation and cultural context of the shipwreck were ascertained.

In April 2011, the excavation of "Xiaobaijiao I" shipwreck was authorized by the State Administration of Cultural Heritage, which became the first formal underwater excavation project in Ningbo as well as in Zhejiang Province, and was one of key programs of national underwater heritage protection in recent years.

From June to July in 2012, the excavation of the antefacts in "Xiaobaijiao I" shipwreck had been accomplished with the effort of underwater archaeologists from all parts of the country who were led by the National Center of Underwater Cultural Heritage and organized by Ningbo Municipal Institute of Cultural Relics and Archaeology (Ningbo Base, National Center of Underwater Cultural Heritage).

In April 2013, the "Xiaobaijiao I" shipwreck Conservation and Restoration Program was authorized by State Administration of Cultural Heritage and formally established.

From May to July in 2014, National Center of Underwater Heritage and Ningbo Municipal

Institute of Cultural Relics and Archaeology (Ningbo Base , National center of Underwater Cultural Heritage) organized another team which was formed by over 20 underwater archaeologists from the world and over 30 experts from several famous institutes to accomplish the task of excavating the shipwreck and protecting the excavation spot.

In October 2014, Ningbo Base, National Center of Underwater Cultural Heritage was established in Chunxiao Town of Beilun District of Ningbo. In the meanwhile, the *Underwater Archaeology in China* exhibition at the Base was opened to display the site replica and some artefacts from "Xiaobaijiao Ⅰ" shipwreck. The ship components of the shipwreck were conserved in the Shipwreck Conservation and Display Area at Ningbo Base to show to the public the results of underwater archaeology and underwater cultural heritage protection. Till then, the excavation project of "Xiaobaijiao Ⅰ" had been successfully completed.

The six-year underwater investigation and excavation manifest that the "Xiaobaijiao Ⅰ" shipwreck is a wooden commercial vessel designed for ocean-going, which sank in Daoguang Reign of Qing Dynasty (1821-1850). The remaining part is about 20.35 meters long and 7.85 meters wide, the wood material of which mainly came from Southeast Asia. A total of over 240 components of the shipwreck have been excavated, including keel, frame, shell, bulkhead, dunnage board, mast base, etc. It is found that "Xiaobaijiao Ⅰ" embodies China's ancient shipbuilding technology and follows foreign shipbuilding traditions in hull structure——a rare tangible example of Chinese shipbuilding technology merging with foreign shipbuilding art.

There are a total of over 1060 artefacts from the "Xiaobaijiao Ⅰ" shipwreck excavation, which include blue-and-white bowls, stem plates, plates, cups, dishes, lamps, lids and spoons, as well as famille verte ceramic bowls, jars, and lids; expert-made Yixing clay teapot, a commercially used jade seal, a wooden stand of inkstone; a calligraphy painting brush; Qing Dynasty Chinese coins, Japanese coins, Vietnamese coins, Spanish silver coins and local-product stone slabs, etc. These precious recovered relics are strong evidence of the impact of the prosperous and lasting "Maritime Silk Road" in Ningbo city, with a high academic value in historical and scientific research.

"Xiaobaijiao Ⅰ" shipwreck excavation concentrated the attention not only for its rich excavated artefacts and integral shipbuilding technology, but also for its advanced working concept, scientific archaeological methods, innovative scientific application, anticipatory protection awareness and multiple security progress. The excavation offers good experiences for the editing of *Regulation of Underwater Archaeological Work (trial version)* which would be soon issued by the State Administration of Cultural Heritage. It was highly prized as "another important mark of development in China from Underwater Archaeology to Underwater Cultural Heritage Protection" and "another Innovative Work in Chinese Underwater Archaeology".

During the excavation of "Xiaobaijiao Ⅰ" shipwreck, a dozen of media institutes reported the project from multi-dimensions and multi-angles. Especially in the 2012 excavation, China Central Television (CCTV) and Ningbo Television (NBTV) broadcasted live shows of "Xiaobaijiao Ⅰ" underwater archaeology for several days in a row. In order to have a profound publicity effect, the State Administration of Cultural Heritage and Zhejiang Provincial Administration of Cultural

Heritage offered a strong support with a great attention; Ningbo municipal Government overall coordinated and organized, and Xiangshan County Government actively collaborated and supported; departments involving propaganda, culture, radio-television, finance, communication, electricity, transport, fishery, maritime safty and meteorology shared the information, collaboratively worked together to assist the live program. Together with the broadcasts of the launch of Shenzhou IX Spaceship and the cruise of Jiaolong Manned Submersible, the live shows of "Xiaobaijiao I" contributed a splendid cultural feast to the public, which made the project a nationwide known event and became an influential propaganda for the famous historical and port city Ningbo.

"Underwater archaeology is a game of chess across the nation". The establishment, implementation and successful completion of "Xiaobaijiao I" project would not be possible without the dedicated support and cooperation from all sides.

We would like to express our gratitude to:

The State Administration of China

Chinese Academy of Cultural Heritage

National Center of Underwater Cultural Heritage

National Museum of China

Zhejiang Provincial Administration of Cultural Heritage

Ningbo Municipal Party Committee, Ningbo Municipal Government

Propaganda Department of Ningbo Municipal Party Committee

Culture, Radio, Television, Press and Publication Bureau of Ningbo

Ningbo Municipal Finance and Tax Bureau

Ningbo Maritime Safety Administration of the People's Republic of China

Ningbo Ocean and Fishery Bureau

Ningbo Port and Shipping Administration

Ningbo Radio and Television Group

Xiangshan County Government, Xiangshan County Standing Committee

Propaganda Department of Xiangshan County Standing Committee

Culture, Radio, Television, Press and Publication Bureau of Xiangshan

Xiangshan Office of Ningbo Maritime Safety Administration of the People's Republic of China

Xiangshan Ocean and Fishery Bureau

Xiangshan Public Security Frontier Forces

Shipu Town Government

Shipu Police Station of Public Security Border Defense

Yushan Village Committee

…

We also would like to express our gratitude to:

(According to the Chinese tradition, the names in this book are in the form with surnames in front of given names)

Deputy Minister of Ministry of Culture, General Director of State Administration of Cultural Heritage   *Li Xiaojie*

Party Member of Ministry of Culture, Curator of Palace Museum   *Shan Jixiang*

Deputy General Director of State Administration of Cultural Heritage   *Tong Mingkang*

Deputy General Director of State Administration of Cultural Heritage   *Gu Yucai*

General Director of Cultural Relics Conservation and Archaeology Department of State Administration of Cultural Heritage   *Guan Qiang*

Deputy Director of Office of State Administration of Cultural Heritage   *Yan Yalin*

Director of Archaeology Division of Cultural Relics Conservation and Archaeology Department of State Administration of Cultural Heritage   *Zhang Lei*

Director of News and Propaganda Division of Policies and Laws Department of State Administration of Cultural Heritage   *Fan Yiran*

Expert of Personnel Department and Director of Training Division of State Administration of Cultural Heritage   *Tong Wei*

Deputy Director of Cultural Relics Division of Cultural Relics Conservation and Archaeology Department of State Administration of Cultural Heritage   *Zhang Ling*

Deputy Director of Archaeology Division of Cultural Relics Conservation and Archaeology Department of State Administration of Cultural Heritage   *Wang Zheng*

Associate Consultant of Archaeology Division of Cultural Relics Conservation and Archaeology Department of State Administration of Cultural Heritage   *Wang Bin*

Head of Chinese Academy of Cultural Heritage   *Liu Shuguang*

Director of National Center of Underwater Cultural Heritage   *Chai Xiaoming*

Party Branch Secretary of National Center of Underwater Cultural Heritage   *Zhang Wei*

Deputy Director of National Center of Underwater Cultural Heritage   *Song Jianzhong*

Assistant Director of National Center of Underwater Cultural Heritage   *Wang Damin*

Director of Underwater Archaeology Department of National Center of Underwater Cultural Heritage   *Jiang Bo*

Director of the Office of National Conservation Center of Underwater Cultural Heritage   *Zhao Jiabin*

Technical Director of National Center of Underwater Cultural Heritage   *Sun Jian*

Deputy Director of Technical and Equipment Department of National Center of Underwater Cultural Heritage   *Li Bin*

Former Inspector of Cultural Department of Zhejiang Province, Former Director of Zhejiang Provincial Administration of Cultural Heritage   *Bao Xianlun*

Deputy General Director of Cultural Department of Zhejiang Province, Director of Zhejiang Provincial Administration of Cultural Heritage   *Chen Yao*

Deputy Inspector of Cultural Department of Zhejiang province, Deputy General Director of Zhejiang Provincial Administration of Cultural Heritage   *Wu Zhiqiang*

Deputy Director General of Zhejiang Provincial Administration of Cultural Heritage   *Zheng Jianhua*

Deputy Director of Zhejiang Provincial Administrationof Cultural Heritage　　Xu Changfeng

Former General Director of Culture, Radio, Television, Press and Publication Bureau of Ningbo　　Chen Jiaqiang

General Director of Culture, Radio, Television, Press and Publication Bureau of Ningbo　　Zhao Huifeng

Deputy General Director of Culture, Radio, Television, Press and Publication Bureau of Ningbo　　Meng Jianyao

Deputy General Director of Culture, Radio, Television, Press and Publication Bureau of Ningbo　　Shu Yueming

Director of Cultural Relics and Museum Department of Culture, Radio, Television, Press and Publication Bureau of Ningbo　　Xu Jiancheng

General Director of Culture, Radio, Television, Press and Publication Bureau of Xiangshan County　　Ren Xianshun

Deputy General Director of Culture, Radio, Television, Press and Publication Bureau of Xiangshan County　　Dong Yun

Director of Cultural Heritage Management Committee Office of Xiangshan County　　Zheng Songcai

"Xiaobaijiao I" Shipwreck Discoverer　　Mou Yonggen

…

Cooperative institutes:

The State Admini stration of Cultural Heritage

Chinese Academy of Science

Peking University

Zhejiang University

Sun Yat-sen Univeristy

Wuhan University of Technology

Guangzhou Salvage Bureau of the Ministry of Transport

Laurel Industrial Company Co., Ltd.

Zhenhai Manyang Co.,Ltd.

Wuhan Hi-Cloud Technology Co., Ltd.

Beijing Guoyang Diving Company

Ningbo Shipu Yushan Aquaculture Co,. Ltd

…

Cooperative individuals:

National Center of Underwater Cultural Heritage	Zhao Jiabin
National Center of Underwater Cultural Heritage	Sun Jian
National Center of Underwater Cultural Heritage	Li Bin
National Center of Underwater Cultural Heritage	Zhou Chunshui
National Center of Underwater Cultural Heritage	Deng Qijiang

National Center of Underwater Cultural Heritage	Meng Yuanzhao
National Center of Underwater Cultural Heritage	E Jie
National Center of Underwater Cultural Heritage	Liang Guoqing
National Center of Underwater Cultural Heritage	Wang Yichen
National Center of Underwater Cultural Heritage	Zhao Zhehao
National Museum of China	Zhu Yanshan
National Museum of China	Qiu Xiuhua
Underwater Archaeology Research and Training Center of National Museum of China	Chen Jianguo
Liaoning Provincial Cultural Relics and Archaeological Research Institute	Feng Lei
Yantai Museum	Sun Zhaofeng
Penglai Municipal Instive of Heritage Management	Zhao Peng
The Chinese Navy Museum	Wang Peng
Nanjing Museum	Wang Qian
Anhui Provincial Cultural Relics and Archaeological Research Institute	Zhang Hui
Fujian Museum	Yang Zelin
Fuzhou Municipal Institute of Cultural Relics and Archaeology	Zhu Bin
Fuzhou Municipal Institute of Cultural Relics and Archaeology	Zhang Yong
Quanzhou Museum	Zhang Hongxing
Zhangzhou Municipal Institute of Cultural Relics and Archaeology	Ruan Yonghao
Ji'an Museum	Zeng Jin
Guangdong Provincial Cultural Relics and Archaeological Research Institute	Li Feiyan
Hainan Museum	Han Fei
Hainan Museum	Cai Fulong (now resign)
Hainan Museum	Huang Kang (now resign)
Eurasia Department of the German Archaeological Institute	Dominic Hosner
Zhoushan Municipal Institute of Cultural Relics	Si Jiuyu
Zhoushan Municipal Institute of Cultural Relics	Ren Jiguo
Heritage Management Committee Office of Xiangshan County	He Junyan
Heritage Management Committee Office of Xiangshan County	Shi Wei
Ningbo Municipal Institute of Cultural Relics and Archaeology	Lin Guocong
Ningbo Municipal Institute of Cultural Relics and Archaeology	Wang Guangyuan
Ningbo Municipal Institute of Cultural Relics and Archaeology	Jin Tao
Ningbo Municipal Institute of Cultural Relics and Archaeology	Luo Peng
Ningbo Municipal Institute of Cultural Relics and Archaeology	Xu Chao
Ningbo Municipal Institute of Cultural Relics and Archaeology	Lei Shao
Ningbo Municipal Institute of Cultural Relics and Archaeology	Li Zechen
Underwater Archaeology Equipment Technician	Fan Kaitai
Underwater Archaeology Equipment Technician	Liu Chunjian
Underwater Archaeology Equipment Technician	Gan Weiyuan

...

On the occasion of the publication, we would like to express sincere gratitude to the above institues, companies and individuals.

Reference

1. Underwater Archaeology Research Centre of National Museum of China, Ningbo Municipal Institute of Cultural Relics and Archaeology, 2011. *Survey and Exploratory Excavation of the "Xiaobaijiao Ⅰ" Shipwreck Site in Yushan. Journal of National Museum of China*.Vol. 11.

2. Ningbo MunicipalInstitute of Cultural Relics and Archaeology, National Center of Underwater Cultural Heritage , 2015. *Brief Excavation Report of Qing Dynasty shipwreck "Xiaobaijiao Ⅰ" in Xiangshan County, Zhejiang Province. Archaeology.* Vol. 6.

3. Ningbo Municipal Institute of Cultural Relics and Archaeology, National Center of Underwater Cultural Heritage, 2014. Another Innovation Work of Underwater Archaeology in China—Shipwreck "Xiaobaijiao Ⅰ" in Ningbo, Zhejiang Province, *China Cultural Relics News*. 29th Aug. p. 5.

4. Lin Guocong and Wang Jiehua, 2015. Management and Innovation for "Xiaobaijiao Ⅰ" Underwater Archaeology Project. In: Lin Guocong and Wang Jiehua. eds., 2015. *New Technologies, New Methods, and New Thoughts: A Collection of the First Ningbo Forum of Underwater Archaeology*. Beijing: Chinese Science Publishing & Media, Ltd.

5. National Center of Underwater Cultural Heritage, Ningbo Institute of Cultural Relics and Archaeology, 2014. *24 Meters Underwater—Record of "Xiaobaijiao Ⅰ" Underwater Archaeology in Xiangshan County, Ningbo, Zhejiang Province*. Beijing: China Broadcasting and Television Press.

Plates 图版

篇章一
青花瓷
Chapter I Blue-and-white Porcelain

"小白礁I号"共计出水青花瓷590件，其中碗526件，豆24件，盘9件，杯25件，碟2件，灯盏1件，盖1件，勺2件。

大多白胎细腻，少量呈灰白色、质地较粗。白釉，多泛青，也有的泛灰白色，釉面多莹润。纹样多为缠枝花卉、花草纹等。青花色泽明艳，有的泛灰。不少青花碗外底心有方形印章式款，有"道光"和"嘉庆"两种底款。

A total of 590 pieces of blue-and-white porcelains were excavated from the "Xiaobaijiao I" shipwreck, including 526 bowls, 24 stem plates, 9 plates, 25 cups, 2 dishes, 1 lamp, 1 lid and 2 spoons.

Bodies of the wares are mostly white and fine, some in grey with relatively coarse textures. Most pieces are glazed white with some shades of blue or grey. The glazes are generally crystal clear, and the patterns are featured with flower scrolls or floral design. The blue-and-white porcelains manifest bright colors, among which some reflect shades of grey. On the bottom of numerous bowls, a type of square-shaped shaped stamp is imprinted in the center, showing the dated inscription of "Daoguang " or "Jiaqing ".

1 嘉庆款青花缠枝花卉纹碗
Blue-and-white Bowl with Dated Inscription of Jiaqing Reign and Flower Scrolls

2014NXXBW1:38

口径17.1cm 底径7.7cm 高7.2cm

Diameter at rim 17.1cm Diameter at footring 7.7cm Height 7.2cm

  敞口，弧腹较深，圈足，制作规整。胎质细白，白釉泛青，釉面莹润，足沿无釉。青花颜色浓重，有晕散效果，纹样线条流畅。口沿内侧绘缠枝花叶纹边饰条带，夹于双弦纹之间，内底心双圈内饰缠枝花叶纹；外壁口沿下饰一周弦纹，腹饰缠枝花叶纹，纹样较密，下腹饰一周变体莲纹，间以双弦纹；圈足外壁饰三周弦纹。外底心有青花篆文方形印章式款，可辨"嘉庆"二字，书写草率。

2 嘉庆款青花缠枝花卉纹碗

Blue–and–white Bowl with Dated Inscription of Jiaqing Reign and Flower Scrolls

2012NXXBW1:122

口径17.4cm 底径7.7cm 高7.2cm

Diameter at rim 17.4cm Diameter at footring 7.7cm Height 7.2cm

　　敞口，弧腹较深，圈足，制作规整。胎质细白，白釉泛青，釉面莹润，足沿无釉。青花颜色浓重，有晕散效果，纹样线条流畅。口沿内侧绘缠枝花叶纹边饰条带，夹于双弦纹之间，内底心双圈内饰缠枝花叶纹；外壁口沿下饰一周弦纹，腹饰缠枝花叶纹，纹样较密，下腹饰一周变体莲纹，间以双弦纹；圈足外壁饰三周弦纹。外底心有青花篆文方形印章式款，可辨"嘉庆"二字，书写草率。

篇章一 青花瓷
Chapter 1 Blue-and-white Porcelain

3 嘉庆款青花缠枝花卉纹碗

Blue-and-white Bowl with Dated Inscription of Jiaqing Reign and Flower Scrolls

2014NXXBW1:10

口径17.3cm 底径7.9cm 高7.0cm

Diameter at rim 17.3cm　Diameter at footring 7.9cm
Height 7.0cm

　　敞口，弧腹较深，圈足，制作规整。胎质细白，白釉泛青，釉面莹润，足沿无釉。青花颜色浓重，有晕散效果，纹样线条流畅。口沿内侧绘缠枝花叶纹边饰条带，夹于双弦纹之间，内底心双圈内饰缠枝花叶纹；外壁口沿下饰一周弦纹，腹饰缠枝花叶纹，纹样较密，下腹饰一周变体莲纹，间以双弦纹；圈足外壁饰三周弦纹。外底心有青花篆文方形印章式款，可辨"嘉庆"二字，书写草率。

Chapter1 Blue-and-white Porcelain 篇章一 青花瓷

23

渔山遗珠——宁波象山『小白礁Ⅰ号』出水文物精品图录

24

4 道光款青花缠枝花卉纹碗

Blue-and-white Bowl with Dated Inscription of Daoguang Reign and Flower Scrolls

2012NXXBW1:42

口径14.5cm 底径6.4cm 高6.5cm

Diameter at rim 14.5cm Diameter at footring 6.4cm Height 6.5cm

  敞口，弧腹较深，圈足，制作规整。胎质细白，白釉泛青，釉面莹润，足沿无釉。青花颜色浓重，有晕散效果，纹样线条流畅。口沿内侧绘缠枝花叶纹边饰条带，夹于双弦纹之间，内底心双圈内饰折枝花卉纹；外壁口沿下饰一周弦纹，腹饰缠枝花叶纹，纹样较密，下腹饰一周变体莲纹，间以双弦纹；圈足外壁饰三周弦纹。外底心有青花篆文方形印章式款，可辨"道光"二字，书写草率。

5 道光款青花缠枝花卉纹碗

Blue-and-white Bowl with Dated Inscription of Daoguang Reign and Flower Scrolls

2012NXXBW1:43

口径14.7cm 底径6.5cm 高6.4cm

Diameter at rim 14.7cm　Diameter at footring 6.5cm　Height 6.4cm

　　敞口，弧腹较深，圈足，制作规整。胎质细白，白釉泛青，釉面莹润，足沿无釉。青花颜色浓重，有晕散效果，纹样线条流畅。口沿内侧绘缠枝花叶纹边饰条带，夹于双弦纹之间，内底心双圈内饰折枝花卉纹；外壁口沿下饰一周弦纹，腹饰缠枝花叶纹，纹样较密，下腹饰一周变体莲纹，间以双弦纹；圈足外壁饰三周弦纹。外底心有青花篆文方形印章式款，可辨"道光"二字，书写草率。

Chapter I Blue-and-white Porcelain 篇章一 青花瓷

27

沧海遗珠
——宁波象山「小白礁Ⅰ号」出水文物精品图录
28

6 嘉庆款青花缠枝花卉纹碗

Blue-and-white Bowl with Dated Inscription of Jiaqing Reign and Flower Scrolls

2012NXXBW1:120

口径14.3cm 底径6.0cm 高6.3cm

Diameter at rim 14.3cm Diameter at footring 6.0cm Height 6.3cm

敞口，弧腹较深，圈足，制作规整。胎质细白，白釉泛青，釉面莹润，足沿无釉。青花颜色浓重，有晕散效果，纹样线条流畅。口沿内侧绘缠枝花叶纹边饰条带，夹于双弦纹之间，内底心双圈内饰折枝花卉纹；外壁口沿下饰一周弦纹，腹饰缠枝花叶纹，纹样较密，下腹饰一周变体莲纹，间以双弦纹；圈足外壁饰三周弦纹。外底心有青花篆文方形印章式款，可辨"嘉庆"二字，书写草率。

7 嘉庆款青花缠枝花卉纹碗

Blue-and-white Bowl with Dated Inscription of Jiaqing Reign and Flower Scrolls

2014NXXBW1:62

口径14.5cm 底径6.4cm 高6.7cm

Diameter at rim 14.5cm Diameter at footring 6.4cm Height 6.7cm

敞口，弧腹较深，圈足，制作规整。胎质细白，白釉泛青，釉面莹润，足沿无釉。青花颜色浓重，有晕散效果，纹样线条流畅。口沿内侧绘缠枝花叶纹边饰条带，夹于双弦纹之间，内底心双圈内饰折枝花卉纹；外壁口沿下饰一周弦纹，腹饰缠枝花叶纹，纹样较密，下腹饰一周变体莲纹，间以双弦纹；圈足外壁饰三周弦纹。外底心有青花篆文方形印章式款，可辨"嘉庆"二字，书写草率。

篇章一 青花瓷
Chapter I Blue-and-white Porcelain

31

8 道光款青花缠枝花卉纹碗
Blue-and-white Bowl with Dated Inscription of Daoguang Reign and Flower Scrolls

2012NXXBW1:21

口径11.5cm 底径5.4cm 高5.3cm

Diameter at rim 11.5cm Diameter at footring 5.4cm Height 5.3cm

敞口，弧腹较深，圈足，制作规整。胎质细白，白釉泛青，釉面莹润，足沿无釉。青花颜色浓重，有晕散效果，纹样线条流畅。口沿内侧绘缠枝花叶纹边饰条带，夹于双弦纹之间，内底心双圈内饰折枝花卉纹；外壁口沿下饰一周弦纹，腹饰缠枝花叶纹，纹样较密；圈足外壁饰三周弦纹。外底心有青花篆文方形印章式款，可辨"道光"二字，书写草率。

9 道光款青花缠枝花卉纹碗
Blue-and-white Bowl with Dated Inscription of Daoguang Reign and Flower Scrolls

2012NXXBW1:24

口径11.6cm 底径5.5cm 高5.5cm

Diameter at rim 11.6cm　Diameter at footring 5.5cm　Height 5.5cm

　　敞口，弧腹较深，圈足，制作规整。胎质细白，白釉泛青，釉面莹润，足沿无釉。青花颜色浓重，有晕散效果，纹样线条流畅。口沿内侧绘缠枝花叶纹边饰条带，夹于双弦纹之间，内底心双圈内饰折枝花卉纹；外壁口沿下饰一周弦纹，腹饰缠枝花叶纹，纹样较密；圈足外壁饰三周弦纹。外底心有青花篆文方形印章式款，可辨"道光"二字，书写草率。

Chapter I Blue-and-white Porcelain 篇章一 青花瓷

35

10 道光款青花缠枝花卉纹碗
Blue-and-white Bowl with Dated Inscription of Daoguang Reign and Flower Scrolls

2014NXXBW1:18

口径11.5cm 底径5.2cm 高5.3cm

Diameter at rim 11.5cm　Diameter at footring 5.2cm　Height 5.3cm

　　敞口，弧腹较深，圈足，制作规整。胎质细白，白釉泛青，釉面莹润，足沿无釉。青花颜色浓重，有晕散效果，纹样线条流畅。口沿内侧绘缠枝花叶纹边饰条带，夹于双弦纹之间，内底心双圈内饰折枝花卉纹；外壁口沿下饰一周弦纹，腹饰缠枝花叶纹，纹样较密；圈足外壁饰三周弦纹。外底心有青花篆文方形印章式款，可辨"道光"二字，书写草率。

11 青花缠枝花卉纹碗
Blue-and-white Bowl with Flower Scrolls

2009NXXBW1:116

口径9.5cm 底径4.6cm 高4.5cm

Diameter at rim 9.5cm Diameter at footring 4.6cm Height 4.5cm

敞口，弧腹较深，圈足，制作规整。胎质细白，白釉泛青，釉面莹润，足沿无釉。青花颜色浓重，有晕散效果，纹样线条流畅。口沿内侧绘缠枝花叶纹边饰条带，夹于双弦纹之间，内底心双圈内饰折枝花卉纹；外壁口沿下饰一周弦纹，腹饰缠枝花叶纹，纹样较密；圈足外壁饰三周弦纹。外底心有青花方形印章式款。

2014NXXBW1:38

2012NXXBW1:42

2012NXXBW1:122

2012NXXBW1:120

2014NXXBW1:38

2012NXXBW1:122

2012NXXBW1:120

2014NXXBW1:62

篇章一　青花瓷

Chapter 1　Blue-and-white Porcelain

2012NXXBW1:120

2014NXXBW1:18

2012NXXBW1:42

2012NXXBW1:24

2012NXXBW1:21

2014NXXBW1:18

2012NXXBW1:43

2012NXXBW1:42

篇章一 青花瓷

Chapter I Blue-and-white Porcelain

12 青花草叶纹碗
Blue-and-white Bowl with Leaves Design

2014NXXBW1:57

口径14.4cm 底径8.8cm 高6.0cm

Diameter at rim 14.4cm　Diameter at footring 8.8cm　Height 6.0cm

　　敞口，斜直腹，圈足，内底涩圈。胎灰白，质较细。白釉泛灰，足沿无釉。青花色泽泛灰。口沿外侧、内底各饰一周弦纹，外腹饰五组草叶纹，圈足外壁饰两周弦纹。

篇章一 青花瓷

Chapter I Blue-and-white Porcelain

45

13 青花花草纹碗
Blue-and-white Bowl with Floral Design

2009NXXBW1:4

口径13.1cm 底径6.8cm 高5.3cm

Diameter at rim 13.1cm　Diameter at footring 6.8cm　Height 5.3cm

　　敞口，斜直腹，圈足，内底涩圈。胎灰白，质较细。白釉泛灰，足沿无釉。青花色泽泛灰，部分呈灰褐色。内底饰青花双弦纹，底心书"二"字，外腹壁饰三朵折枝花卉。

篇章一 青花瓷

Chapter1 Blue-and-white Porcelain

47

宁波象山『小白礁Ⅰ号』出水文物精品图录 48

14 青花花草纹碗
Blue-and-white Bowl with Floral Design

2009NXXBW1:5

口径12.9cm 底径7.2cm 高4.5cm

Diameter at rim 12.9cm Diameter at footring 7.2cm Height 4.5cm

　　敞口，斜直腹，圈足，内底涩圈。胎灰白，质较细。白釉泛灰，足沿无釉。青花色泽泛灰，部分呈灰褐色。内底饰青花双弦纹，外腹壁饰三朵折枝花卉。

15 青花花草纹碗
Blue-and-white Bowl with Floral Design

2014NXXBW1:2

口径13.0cm 底径7.0cm 高4.8cm

Diameter at rim 13.0cm Diameter at footring 7.0cm Height 4.8cm

敞口，斜直腹，圈足，内底涩圈。胎灰白，质较细。白釉泛灰，足沿无釉。青花色泽泛灰，部分呈灰褐色。口沿内侧饰一周弦纹，内底饰青花双弦纹，内边缘书"二"字；外壁口沿下饰一周弦纹，腹饰三朵折枝花卉。器表有贝类附着物。

篇章一　青花瓷

Chapter 1　Blue-and-white Porcelain

16 青花竖线纹碗

Blue-and-white Bowl with Linear Pattern

2014NXXBW1:116

口径12.2cm 底径6.6cm 高4.6cm
Diameter at rim 12.2cm Diameter at footring 6.6cm Height 4.6cm

　　敞口,斜直腹,圈足。内底涩圈,外底心有脐突。胎灰白,质较细。白釉泛灰,足底无釉。青花色泽泛灰。内底饰一周青花粗弦纹,外壁口沿下饰双弦纹,间饰竖线纹,线条随意且较粗。

17 青花折线纹碗
Blue-and-white Bowl with Wave Pattern

2014NXXBW1: 78

口径12.5cm 底径5.8cm 高4.0cm

Diameter at rim 12.5cm Diameter at footring 5.8cm Height 4.0cm

敞口，斜直腹，圈足。内底涩圈，外底心有脐突。胎灰白，质较酥。白釉泛灰，足底无釉。青花色泽泛灰。内底饰一周青花粗弦纹，底心饰一圆圈，笔法草率；外壁口沿下饰三组平行折线纹；腹底部与圈足间饰两周弦纹。

18 青花灵芝纹碗

Blue-and-white Bowl with Fungus Design

2014NXXBW1:61

口径16.8cm 底径7.4cm 高7.8cm

Diameter at rim 16.8cm Diameter at footring 7.4cm Height 7.8cm

敞口，弧腹较深，圈足。胎质细白，白釉泛青，釉面莹润，足沿无釉。青花色泽艳丽。内腹壁饰满灵芝纹，内底饰一周葵纹，底心饰一朵折枝花卉；外腹壁亦饰满灵芝纹；圈足外壁饰三周弦纹，外底心饰双弦纹，内有青花方形印章式款。

篇章一　青花瓷

Chapter I Blue-and-white Porcelain

——宁波象山『小白礁Ⅰ号』出水文物精品图录

19 青花灵芝纹碗
Blue-and-white Bowl with Fungus Design

2014NXXBW1:63

口径13.7cm 底径6.3cm 高6.7cm

Diameter at rim 13.7cm　Diameter at footring 6.3cm　Height 6.7cm

　　敞口，弧腹较深，圈足。胎质细白，白釉泛青，釉面莹润，足沿无釉。青花色泽艳丽。内底饰双弦纹，底心饰一朵折枝花卉，外腹壁饰满灵芝纹，外底心饰双弦纹，内有青花方形印章式款。

20 青花花草纹菱口豆
Blue-and-white Lobed Stem Plate with Floral Design

2014NXXBW1:40

口径11.6m 底径5.9cm 高5.0cm

Diameter at rim 11.5cm Diameter at footring 6.5cm Height 4.7cm

菱口，折沿，浅弧腹，盘心较平，高圈足外撇。胎质细白，白釉泛青，釉面莹润，足沿无釉。青花色泽鲜艳，有晕散效果。盘沿、内外腹部饰十五组花草纹；内底心饰莲子纹；圈足外壁饰三道弦纹，第一、二道弦纹之间饰有条带状纹样。

21 青花花草纹菱口豆
Blue-and-white Lobed Stem Plate with Floral Design

2014NXXBW1:64

口径11.5cm 底径6.0cm 高5.0cm

Diameter at rim 11.5cm Diameter at footring 6.0cm Height 5.0cm

　　菱口，折沿，浅弧腹，盘心较平，高圈足外撇。胎质细白，白釉泛青，釉面莹润，足沿无釉。青花色泽鲜艳，有晕散效果。盘沿、内外腹部饰十五组花草纹；内底心饰莲子纹；圈足外壁饰四道弦纹，第二、三道弦纹之间饰有条带状纹样。

篇章一 青花瓷

Chapter I Blue-and-white Porcelain

——宁波象山「小白礁Ⅰ号」出水文物精品图录

22 青花花草纹菱口豆
Blue-and-white Lobed Stem Plate with Floral Design

2012NXXBW1:71

口径11.0cm 底径6.2cm 高5.0cm

Diameter at rim 11.0cm Diameter at footring 6.2cm Height 5.0cm

菱口，折沿，浅弧腹，盘心较平，高圈足外撇。胎质细白，白釉泛青，釉面莹润，足沿无釉。青花色泽鲜艳，有晕散效果。盘沿、内腹部饰青花地纹，内底心饰花草纹；外腹饰十五组花草纹，其下为放射状直线纹。圈足饰上下双弦纹，中间饰芭蕉叶纹。

23 青花花草纹菱口豆
Blue-and-white Lobed Stem Plate with Floral Design

2014NXXBW1:15

口径11.0cm 底径6.5cm 高5.2cm

Diameter at rim 11.0cm Diameter at footring 6.5cm Height 5.2cm

菱口，折沿，浅弧腹，盘心较平，高圈足外撇。胎质细白，白釉泛青，釉面莹润，足沿无釉。青花色泽鲜艳，有晕散效果。盘沿、内腹部饰青花地纹，内底心饰花草纹；外腹饰十五组花草纹，其下为放射状直线纹。圈足饰上下双弦纹，中间饰芭蕉叶纹。

24 青花花草纹菱口豆

Blue-and-white Lobed Stem Plate with Floral Design

2014NXXBW1:55

口径11.7cm 底径6.3cm 高4.9cm

Diameter at rim 11.7cm　Diameter at footring 6.3cm　Height 4.9cm

菱口，折沿，浅弧腹，盘心较平，高圈足外撇。胎质细白，白釉泛青，釉面莹润，足沿无釉。青花色泽鲜艳，有晕散效果。盘沿、内腹部饰青花地纹，内底心饰花草纹；外腹饰十六组花草纹，其下为放射状直线纹。圈足饰上下双弦纹，中间饰芭蕉叶纹。

——宁波象山【小白礁Ⅰ号】出水文物精品图录

25 青花花草纹菱口豆
Blue-and-white Lobed Stem Plate with Floral Design

2014NXXBW1:41

口径11.0cm 底径6.0cm 高5.0cm

Diameter at rim 11.0cm Diameter at footring 6.0cm Height 5.0cm

  菱口，折沿，浅弧腹，盘心较平，高圈足外撇。胎质细白，白釉泛青，釉面莹润，足沿无釉。青花色泽鲜艳，有晕散效果。盘沿、内腹部饰青花地纹，内底心饰花草纹；外腹饰十五组花草纹，其下为放射状直线纹。圈足饰上下双弦纹，中间饰芭蕉叶纹。

26 青花花草纹菱口豆

Blue-and-white Lobed Stem Plate with Floral Design

2014NXXBW1:42

口径11.0cm 底径6.0cm 高5.0cm

Diameter at rim 11.0cm Diameter at footring 6.0cm
Height 5.0cm

　　菱口，折沿，浅弧腹，盘心较平，高圈足外撇。胎质细白，白釉泛青，釉面莹润，足沿无釉。青花色泽鲜艳，有晕散效果。盘沿、内腹部饰青花地纹，内底心饰花草纹；外腹饰十五组花草纹，其下为放射状直线纹。圈足饰上下双弦纹，中间饰芭蕉叶纹。

篇章一　青花瓷
Chapter I　Blue-and-white Porcelain

⑦¹

2014NXXBW1:40

2012NXXBW1:71

2014NXXBW1:55

2014NXXBW1:41

2014NXXBW1:40

2014NXXBW1:64

2012NXXBW1:71

2014NXXBW1:55

篇章一 青花瓷

Chapter I Blue-and-white Porcelain

27 青花灵芝纹盘
Blue-and-white Plate with Fungus Design

2012NXXBW1:81

口径15.1cm 底径9.6cm 高2.7cm

Diameter at rim 15.1cm Diameter at footring 9.6cm Height 2.7cm

　　敞口，圆唇，斜弧腹，圈足。胎质细白，白釉泛青，釉面莹润，足沿无釉。青花色泽艳丽。内腹饰满灵芝纹；内底边缘饰一周葵纹，底心饰一朵折枝花卉；外腹饰三朵折枝花卉；外底饰双弦纹，中心绘青花方形印章式款。

28 青花菊瓣纹"福"款盘
Blue-and-white Plate with Chrysanthemum Petal and *Fu* Inscription

2012NXXBW1:78

口径16.0cm 底径9.3cm 高3.6cm

Diameter at rim 16.0cm　Diameter at footring 9.3cm

Height 3.6cm

　　敞口，圆唇，斜弧腹，圈足。内底涩圈，外底心有脐突。胎灰白，质较细。釉色青白，釉层较厚，外足端刮釉。青花色泽泛灰。内腹饰双弦纹，夹于双弦纹之间绘一周菊瓣纹；内底心书"福"字，边饰一周弦纹；外腹口沿下饰一周弦纹，圈足外壁饰两周弦纹。

29 青花菊瓣纹"福"款盘

Blue-and-white Plate with Chrysanthemum Petal and *Fu* Inscription

2012NXXBW1:79

口径15.5cm 底径9.3cm 高3.7cm

Diameter at rim 15.5cm Diameter at footring 9.3cm Height 3.7cm

敞口，圆唇，斜弧腹，圈足。内底涩圈，外底心有脐突。胎灰白，质较细。釉色青白，釉层较厚，外足无釉。青花色泽泛灰。内腹饰三道弦纹，夹于第一、二道弦纹之间绘一周菊瓣纹；内底心书"福"字，字迹潦草，边饰一涩圈；口沿外侧、下腹及圈足外壁各饰一周弦纹。

30 青花草叶纹盘
Blue-and-white Plate with Leaves Design

2008NXXBW1:4

口径17.2cm 底径8.7cm 高4.2cm

Diameter at rim 17.2cm　Diameter at footring 8.7cm
Height 4.2cm

　　敞口，斜弧腹，圈足。内底涩圈，外底心有脐突。胎灰白，质较细。釉色青白，釉层较厚，外足端刮釉。青花色泽泛灰。内外腹及内底饰草叶纹。器表有贝类附着物。

篇章一 青花瓷
Chapter I Blue-and-white Porcelain

渔山遗珠——宁波象山「小白礁一号」出水文物精品图录

80

31 青花缠枝花卉纹杯
Blue-and-white Cup with Flower Scrolls

2009NXXBW1:81

口径6.7cm 底径3.5cm 高5.2cm

Diameter at rim 6.7cm Diameter at footring 3.5cm
Height 5.2cm

敞口，弧腹较深，圈足，制作规整。胎质细白，白釉泛青，釉面莹润，足沿无釉。青花颜色浓重，有晕散效果，纹样线条流畅。口沿内侧绘缠枝花叶纹边饰条带，夹于双弦纹之间；内底心双圈内饰折枝花卉纹；外壁口沿下饰一周弦纹，腹饰缠枝花叶纹，纹样较密；圈足外壁饰一周弦纹，外底心有青花方形印章式款。

32 青花缠枝花卉纹杯
Blue-and-white Cup with Flower Scrolls

2014NXXBW1:138

口径6.9cm 底径2.7cm 高5.5cm

Diameter at rim 6.9cm Diameter at footring 2.7cm Height 5.5cm

敞口，深弧腹，圈足，制作规整。胎质细白，白釉泛青，釉面莹润，足沿无釉。青花色泽明艳，纹样线条流畅。外壁口沿下饰两周弦纹，腹壁饰满缠枝花卉纹，圈足外壁饰一周弦纹。

33 青花缠枝花卉纹碟
Blue-and-white Dish with Flower Scrolls

2014NXXBW1:119

口径8.8cm 底径4.5cm 高2.5cm

Diameter at rim 8.8cm Diameter at footring 4.5cm Height 2.5cm

　　侈口，斜弧腹，圈足，制作规整。胎质细白，白釉泛青，釉面莹润，足沿无釉。青花颜色浓重，晕散明显，纹样线条流畅。口沿外侧绘双弦纹，外壁绘缠枝花卉纹，圈足外壁饰一周弦纹。内壁饰青花地纹，内底饰满缠枝花叶纹，边缘饰两周弦纹。

34 青花缠枝花草纹灯盏
Blue-and-white Lamp with Floral Scrolls

2008NXXBW1: 16

灯盘口径5.1cm 底径4.1cm 灯台口径10.5cm 底径6.8cm 通高10.5cm

Upper disc: Upper Diameter 5.1cm Lower Diameter 4.1cm

Lower disc: Upper Diameter 10.5cm Lower Diameter 6.8cm

Overall height 10.5cm

灯盘撇口，折腹，盘心平。灯柱呈细长圆台状，上细，下粗，中空，把残。灯台呈盘状，侈口，盘心平，矮圈足。胎质细白，白釉泛青，釉面莹润，外底无釉。青花色泽明艳，纹样线条流畅。灯盘、灯台饰卷云纹、卷草纹、花草纹，灯柱上饰缠枝花草纹，下饰芭蕉叶纹。

Chapter I Blue-and-white Porcelain 篇章一 青花瓷

85

35 青花缠枝花卉纹盖

Blue-and-white Lid with Flower Scrolls

2009NXXBW1:12

口径9.9cm 钮径4.0cm 高3.5cm

Diameter at rim 9.9cm Diameter of the handle 4.0cm Height 3.5cm

略呈覆碗状，敞口，弧腹较浅，盖面隆起，圈足状圆钮。胎质细白，白釉泛青，釉面莹润。青花色泽明艳，纹样线条流畅。钮外边缘饰一周弦纹；盖面饰满缠枝花卉纹，线条较细；近口部饰两周弦纹。钮内有青花篆文方形印章式款，可辨"嘉庆"二字，字迹草率。

36 青花缠枝花草纹勺
Blue-and-white Spoon with Floral Scrolls

2014NXXBW1:7

长11.5cm 宽5.2cm 高4.3cm

Length11.5cm Width 5.2cm Height 4.3cm

　　敞口，直柄，平底内凹。胎质细白，白釉泛青，釉面莹润，足底刮釉。青花颜色浓重，晕散明显，纹样线条流畅。勺内侧饰缠枝花草纹，外底心有青花方形印章式款。

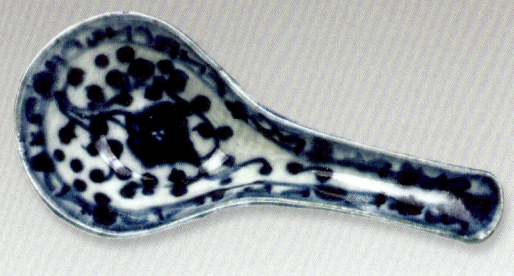

37 青花缠枝花草纹勺
Blue-and-white Spoon with Floral Scrolls

2014NXXBW1:101

长11.6cm 宽5.3cm 高4.3cm

Length 11.6cm Width 5.3cm Height 4.3cm

敞口，直柄，平底内凹。胎质细白，白釉泛青，釉面莹润，足底刮釉。青花颜色浓重，晕散明显，纹样线条流畅。勺内侧饰缠枝花草纹，外底心有青花方形印章式款。

篇章二
五彩瓷

Chapter II Famille Verte Porcelain

"小白礁I号"共出水五彩瓷44件,其中碗3件,罐7件,盖34件。

大多白胎细腻,白釉泛青,釉面莹润。因海水浸泡、侵蚀,器表色彩脱落严重,可辨有绿、黑、黄、红等色,图案模糊难辨。器表有贝类附着物。

A total of 44 pieces of Famille Verte porcelains were excavated from the "Xiaobaijiao I" shipwreck, including 3 bowls, 7 jars and 34 lids.

Most pieces possess white and fine bodies, white glazes with shades of blue and crystal clear surfaces. Soaked and corroded in seawater, colors on the surface of the porcelain wares have been severely damaged. Some colors, such as green, black, yellow and red, are still distinguishable, while the patterns are ambiguous with shellfish attached onto the surface of the artefacts.

1 五彩碗
Famille Verte Bowl

2012NXXBW1:82

口径14.6cm 底径5.9cm 高8.3cm

Diameter at rim 14.6cm Diameter at footring 5.9cm Height 8.3cm

敞口，深弧腹，圈足。白胎细腻，白釉泛青，釉面莹润，足沿无釉。口沿内外侧分别饰一周条带状黄色、绿色图案，内外腹分别有蓝色、黑色图案残迹，内底饰绿色葵花纹。因海水浸泡、侵蚀，器表色彩脱落严重，图案模糊难辨，有贝类附着物。

2 五彩碗
Famille Verte Bowl

2012NXXBW1:83

口径15.1cm 底径6.1cm 高8.1cm

Diameter at rim 15.1cm Diameter at footring 6.1cm Height 8.1cm

敞口，深弧腹，圈足。白胎细腻，白釉泛青，釉面莹润，足沿无釉。口沿内外侧各有一周条带状彩色图案，外腹可见彩色图案残迹。因海水浸泡、侵蚀，器表色彩脱落严重，图案模糊难辨，有较多贝类附着物。

3 五彩盖罐
Famille Verte Jar

2009NXXBW1:16（盖） 2009NXXBW1:27（罐）

盖 口径12.5cm 沿径17.3cm 高8.0cm

罐 口径15.7cm 底径12.0cm 高10.8cm

通高18.5cm

Lid: Inner diameter 12.5cm Outer diameter 17.3cm Height 8.0cm

Jar: Diameter at rim 15.7cm Diameter at footring 12.0cm Height 10.8cm

Overall height 18.5cm

　　盖　子口，盖沿外折，盖面隆起，双层塔式宝珠钮。白胎细腻，盖内沿无釉。盖面纹饰图案模糊不清，仅部分色彩仍旧鲜艳亮丽，可辨颜色有绿色、黑色。器表有贝类附着物。

　　罐　芒口，母口，斜直腹微弧，圈足。白胎细腻，足沿内外刮削无釉。罐身口沿下有一周连珠纹残迹，外腹壁密布绿色图案。器表有贝类附着物。

篇章二 Famille Verte Porcelain

——宁波象山『小白礁Ⅰ号』出水文物精品图录
96

4 五彩盖罐
Famille Verte Jar

2009NXXBW1:474（盖） 2009NXXBW1:475（罐）

盖 口径12.1cm 沿径15.3cm 高7.5cm

罐 口径14.4cm 底径8.7cm 高10.3cm

通高17.5cm

Lid: Inner diameter 12.2cm Outer diameter 15.3 cm Height 7.5cm

Jar: Diameter at rim 14.4cm Diameter at footring 8.7cm Height 10.3cm

Overall height 17.5cm

　　盖　子口，盖沿外折，盖面隆起，双层塔式宝珠钮。白胎细腻，盖内沿无釉。盖面纹饰图案模糊不清，可见黑色斑块。器表有贝类附着物。

　　罐　芒口，母口，斜直腹微弧，圈足。白胎细腻，足沿内外刮削无釉。罐身口沿下和腹底部饰一周连珠纹，外腹壁密布绿色图案或残迹。器表有贝类附着物。

5 五彩盖罐
Famille Verte Jar

2009NXXBW1:25（盖） 2014NXXBW1: 449（罐）

盖 口径8.3cm 沿径10.8cm 高5.1cm

罐 口径9.9cm 底径6.0cm 高7.0cm

通高12.0cm

Lid: Inner diameter 8.3cm Outer diameter 10.8cm Height 5.1cm

Jar: Diameter at rim 9.9cm Diameter at footring 6.0cm Height 7.0cm

Overall height 12.0cm

　　盖 子口，盖沿外折，盖面隆起，双层塔式宝珠钮。白胎细腻，盖内沿无釉。盖面纹饰图案模糊不清，可见绿色斑块。器表有贝类附着物。

　　罐 芒口，母口，斜直腹微弧，圈足。白胎细腻，足沿内外刮削无釉。罐身口沿下饰一周连珠纹，外腹壁密布黑色绿色图案或残迹。器表有少量贝类附着物。

篇章二 五彩瓷

Chapter II Famille Verte Porcelain

6 五彩器盖
Famille Verte Lid

2012NXXBW1:88

口径14.0cm 沿径17.2cm 高9.3cm

Inner diameter 14.0cm Outer diameter 17.2cm Height 9.3cm

　　子口，盖沿外折，盖面隆起，双层塔式宝珠钮。白胎细腻，盖内沿无釉。盖面绘饰图案模糊不清，可见墨绿色斑块。器表有贝类附着物。

7 五彩器盖
Famille Verte Lid

2009NXXBW1:20

口径12.4cm 沿径15.0cm 高7.8cm

Inner diameter 12.4cm Outer diameter 15.0cm Height 7.8cm

　　子口，盖沿外折，盖面隆起，双层塔式宝珠钮。白胎细腻，盖内沿无釉。盖面绘饰图案模糊不清，仅见少量绿色斑块。器表有贝类附着物。

8 五彩器盖
Famille Verte Lid

2009NXXBW1:23

口径10.7cm 沿径13.5cm 高6.8cm

Inner diameter10.7cm Outer diameter 13.5cm Height 6.8cm

　　残，子口，盖沿外折，盖面隆起，双层塔式宝珠钮。白胎细腻，盖内沿无釉。盖面绘饰图案模糊不清，仅见残迹。器表有贝类附着物。

9 五彩器盖
Famille Verte Lid

2014NXXBW1:100

口径9.3cm 沿径12.2cm 高6.1cm

Inner diameter 9.3cm Outer diameter 12.2cm Height 6.1cm

子口，盖沿外折，盖面隆起，双层塔式宝珠钮。白胎细腻，盖内沿无釉。盖面绘饰图案模糊不清，可见墨色斑块。器表有贝类附着物。

10 五彩器盖
Famille Verte Lid

2012NXXBW1:86

口径8.5cm 沿径10.0cm 高5.6cm

Inner diameter 8.5cm Outer diameter 10.0cm Height 5.6cm

  子口，盖沿外折，盖面隆起，双层塔式宝珠钮。白胎细腻，盖内沿无釉。盖面绘饰图案模糊不清，仅见黑色残迹。器表有贝类附着物。

篇章三
陶器
Chapter III Pottery

"小白礁Ⅰ号"共出水陶器17件,其中紫砂壶1件、罐1件,酱釉陶罐8件、壶3件、盖2件、盆1件、缸1件。

A total of 17 pieces of pottery were excavated from the "XiaobaijiaoⅠ" shipwreck, including 1 Yixing clay teapot and 1 Yixing clay jar, 8 brown glazed ewers, 3 ewers, 2 lids, 1 basin and 1 vat.

1 紫砂壶
Yixing Clay Teapot

2012NXXBW1:91

口径6.2cm 底径6.9cm 高4.3cm

Diameter at rim 6.2cm Diameter at footring 6.9cm Height 4.3cm

红胎，胎质细腻。敛口，方沿，折弧腹，平底微内凹，有流，有把，盖失。素面无纹。底款书"二水中分白鹭洲 孟臣制"。

篇章三 陶器
Chapter III Pottery

2 紫砂罐
Yixing Clay Jar

2014NXXBW1: 60

口径2.5cm 底径5.0cm 高6.5cm

Diameter at rim 2.5cm Diameter at footring 5.0cm Height 6.5cm

红胎，胎质细腻。敛口，方沿，短颈，溜肩，鼓腹，圈足，平底。素面无纹。

渔山遗珠
——宁波象山『小白礁Ⅰ号』出水文物精品图录

112

3 酱釉陶壶
Brown Glazed Ewer

2009NXXBW1: 31

口径8.5cm 底径10.7cm 高16.8cm

Diameter at rim 8.5cm Diameter at footring 10.7cm Height 16.8cm

敛口，圆唇，束颈，斜弧腹，平底内凹，流上部与颈肩有粘接。酱黑釉，内口沿有釉，内腹无釉。

4 酱釉陶壶
Brown Glazed Ewer

2012NXXBW1:90

口径11.0cm 底径11.0cm 高21.9cm

Diameter at rim 11.0cm Diameter at footring 11.0cm Height 21.9cm

侈口，圆唇，束颈较短，鼓腹，平底内凹，有流，无把。灰褐胎，较粗糙。酱灰釉，外底无釉。器表有贝类附着物。

5 酱釉陶罐
Brown Glazed Jar

2008NXXBW1:9

口径11.5cm 底径17.0cm 高14.7cm

Diameter at rim 11.5cm Diameter at footring 17.0cm Height 14.7cm

　　圆唇，直口，口沿外凸，折肩，斜直腹，平底内凹。肩部和上腹饰竖线纹。灰褐胎，较粗糙。酱绿釉，外底无釉。器表有贝类附着物。

6 酱釉四系陶罐
Brown Glazed Jar with Four Rings

2014NXXBW1:30

口径11.7cm 底径17.0cm 高30.3cm

Diameter at rim 11.7cm　Diameter at footring 17.0cm　Height 30.3cm

敞口，束颈，四系，肩上有脊，鼓腹，平底。浅红胎，较粗糙。酱褐釉，釉不及底。器表有贝类附着物。

7 酱釉陶罐
Brown Glazed Jar

2014NXXBW1:103

口径10.5cm 底径9.6cm 高15.8cm

Diameter at rim 10.5cm Diameter at footring 9.6cm Height 15.8cm

敞口，圆唇，束颈，弧腹，圈足，平底。红褐胎，较粗糙，胎体厚重。酱红釉，外底无釉。器底有贝类附着物。

8 酱釉陶罐
Brown Glazed Jar

2014NXXBW1:105

口径11.2cm 底径9.3cm 高8.4cm

Diameter at rim 11.2cm Diameter at footring 9.3cm Height 8.4cm

子口，直腹内斜，平底。施釉至肩部，外底无釉。红灰胎，胎质较硬。酱褐釉，釉不及底。器表有贝类附着物。

9 酱釉凤穿牡丹花卉纹子口盖

Brown Glazed Lid with Phoenix amid Peony Scrolls

2012NXXBW1:89

口径14.3 沿径19.1cm 高2.1cm

Inner diameter 14.3cm　Outer diameter 19.1cm　Height 2.1cm

灰胎，夹粗砂。酱褐色釉，正面满釉，背面无釉。圆形状，盖面中心泥条堆塑桥形钮，背面近边缘处泥条堆塑一周成子口。盖面近边缘处压印一周花卉纹，内有凤穿牡丹纹；背面压印乳钉纹。器表有贝类附着物。

篇章四
金属器
Chapter IV Metal Artefact

"小白礁Ⅰ号"共出水金属器74件，其中测深铅锤1件，铅片2件，银饼2块，银币1枚，铜钱57枚，铜螺栓4件，铜盖1件，锡砚1件，其他金属构件5件。

A total of 74 pieces of metal artefacts were excavated from the "Xiaobaijiao Ⅰ" shipwreck, including 1 sounding lead, 2 lead pieces, 2 discoid silvers, 1 silver coin, 57 copper coins, 4 copper bolts, 1 copper lid, 1 tin inkstone and 5 other metal components.

1 测深铅锤
Sounding Lead

2014NXXBW1:65

底径4.0cm 高9.3cm

Diameter at bottom 4.0cm Height 9.3cm

铅锡合金。圆锥状，上细下粗，顶端残，近顶端有一圆孔，用于穿绳。器表锈蚀，有贝类附着物。用于行船测量水深。

2 银饼
Discoid Silver

2014NXXBW1:450

直径4.2cm 厚1.0cm

Diameter 4.2cm Thickness 1.0cm

银质。圆饼状。灰黑色。器表粗糙，表面有杂质。

3 西班牙银币
Spanish Silver Coin

2008NXXBW1:11

直径3.9cm 厚0.2cm

Diameter 3.9cm Thickness 0.2cm

银质，圆形，边缘压花，表面磨损，图案模糊。正面图案、印文模糊难辨，应为头像和铸造年代；背面是王冠、盾徽，两边双柱，周围镌刻西班牙文"HISPAN.ET IND.REX.M.8R. F.M"，并戳印有不同样式的字符。

4 康熙通宝
Kangxi Tongbao Coin

2009NXXBW1:39

直径2.6cm 孔边长0.5cm 郭宽0.3cm 厚0.1cm

Diameter 2.6cm Side length at hole 0.5cm Edeg width 0.3cm Thickness 0.1cm

黄铜，圆形方孔，带边郭。面文"康熙通宝"，背文为满文。表面有铜锈。铸于清圣祖康熙年间（1662—1722）。

5 雍正通宝
Yongzheng Tongbao Coin

2014NXXBW1:96

直径2.5cm 孔边长0.5cm 郭宽0.3cm 厚0.1cm

Diameter 2.5cm Side length at hole 0.5cm Edge width 0.3cm Thickness 0.1cm

  黄铜，圆形方孔，带边郭。面文"雍正通宝"，背文为满文。表面有铜锈。铸于清世宗雍正年间（1723—1735）。

6 乾隆通宝
Qianlong Tongbao Coin

2009NXXBW1:57

直径2.3cm 孔边长0.6cm 郭宽0.3cm 厚0.1cm
Diameter 2.3cm Side length at hole 0.6cm Edge width 0.3cm Thickness 0.1cm

黄铜，圆形方孔，带边郭。面文"乾隆通宝"，背文为满文。表面有铜锈。铸于清高宗乾隆年间（1736—1795）。

7 嘉庆通宝
Jiaqing Tongbao Coin

2009NXXBW1:70

直径2.2cm 孔边长0.5cm 郭宽0.2cm 厚 0.1cm

Diameter 2.2cm Side length at hole 0.5cm Edge width 0.2cm Thickness 0.1cm

　　黄铜，圆形方孔，带边郭。面文"嘉庆通宝"，背文为满文。表面有铜锈。铸于清仁宗嘉庆年间（1796—1820）。

8 道光通宝
Daoguang Tongbao Coin

2009NXXBW1:76

直径2.3cm 孔边长0.5cm 郭宽0.2cm 厚0.1cm

Diameter 2.3cm Side length at hole 0.5cm Edge width 0.2cm Thickness 0.1cm

  黄铜，圆形方孔，带边郭。面文"道光通宝"，背文为满文。表面有铜锈。铸于清宣宗道光年间（1821—1850）。

9 宽永通宝
Kan'ei Tongbao Coin

2009NXXBW1:78

直径2.2cm 孔边长0.7cm 郭宽0.2cm 厚0.1cm

Diameter 2.2cm Side length at hole 0.7cm Edge width 0.2cm Thickness 0.1cm

　　黄铜，圆形方孔，带边郭。表面锈蚀严重，可辨面文"宽永通宝"。

　　宽永通宝始铸于日本第108代后水尾天皇宽永三年（1626），从1636年开始大量铸造，流通时间长240余年。宽永通宝在长期的中日贸易及交往中不断流入我国，至今在我国各地均有发现。

10 景兴通宝
King Hing Tongbao Coin

2009NXXBW1:77

直径2.3cm 孔边长0.6cm 郭宽0.3cm 厚0.1cm

Diameter 2.3cm Side length at hole 0.6cm Edge width 0.3cm
Thickness 0.1cm

  黄铜，圆形方孔，带边郭。表面锈蚀严重，可辨面文"景兴通宝"。

  景兴通宝铸于后黎朝显宗黎维禟景兴年间（1740—1777），时值清乾隆五至四十二年，为安南（越南的旧称）货币史上流通时间最长、品种最多、数量最大的一种钱币。景兴通宝在长期的中越贸易及交往中不断流入我国，至今在我国各地均有发现。

11 铜螺栓
Copper Bolt

2014NXXBW1:3

头部直径1.3cm 长 5.3cm

Diameter 1.3cm Length 5.3cm

黄铜质。由头部和螺杆组成；头部为圆形，正中与螺杆嵌接；螺杆上粗下细，上部横截面为方形，下部横截面为圆形，底端有螺纹。器表有铜锈。

12 铜盖
Copper Cover

2008NXXBW1:14

口径7.9cm 高0.9cm

Diameter at rim 7.9cm Height 0.9cm

黄铜质，器表泛铜绿。口沿残，圆形。口沿平，圆弧面。

渔山遗珠——宁波象山『小白礁一号』出水文物精品图录

134

13 陀螺状铜构件
Turbinated Copper Element

2012NXXBW1:93

最宽4.2cm 通高 4.5cm

Width 4.2cm Height 4.5cm

  黄铜质，灰黑色，表面锈蚀。陀螺状，分为上、下两部分；上部为塔式带针状；下部为折腹圆台状，中通圆孔。

篇章五
其他器物
Chapter V Other Artefact

"小白礁I号"还出水印章1方、毛笔1支、砚台底座1件、石板材331块、砺石1件、砖头3块、焦炭若干。

There are 1 seal, 1 calligraphy painting brush, 1 inkstone stand, 331 stone slabs, 1 grindstone, 3 bricks and several charcoals excavated from the "Xiaobaijiao I" shipwreck.

1 "源合盛记"印章
Seal with *Yuan He Sheng Ji* Inscription

2008NXXBW1:12

边长2.7cm 高3.1cm

Side Length 2.7cm   Height 3.1cm

叶腊石，正四棱柱状。印面正方形，双边框。阳刻楷体反纹"源合盛记"；顶面刻"上"字，与底面印文字方向相同。

2 毛笔
Calligraphy Painting Brush

2014NXXBW1:68

笔杆长19.5cm 直径1.2cm 笔头长2.5cm 通长22.0cm

Length of penholder 19.5cm Diameter 1.2cm

Length of pen point 2.5cm Overall height 22.0cm

由笔杆与笔头组成。笔杆为圆柱状，竹制，中空。笔头为椭圆状，笔锋磨损严重，残留有朱砂痕迹。

3 砚台底座
Inkstone Stand

2014NXXBW1:1
长15.0cm 宽11.0cm 高1.6cm
Length 15.0cm Width 11.0cm Height 1.6cm

木质。近似椭圆状。子口，平底内凹，四矮足。内底平直，起泡，开裂，有划痕；外底心平直。

4 石板
Stone Slab

2014NXXBW1:371

长81.0cm 宽60.0cm 高7.0cm

Length 81.0cm Width 60.0cm Height 7.0cm

薄长方体，质地均匀细密，色泽微红。粗加工，器表凹凸不平，有贝类等附着物。

篇章六
船体构件
Chapter VI　Ship Structural Component

"小白礁Ⅰ号"船体残长约20.35米，残宽约7.85米；出水船体构件244件，包括龙骨3件、船壳板94件、肋骨63件、肋骨补强材7件、肋骨连接板11件、隔舱板3件、隔舱板加强材1件、压条6件、铺舱板37件、桅座1件、顶杠1件、散件17件。

The remaining part of "Xiaobaijiao Ⅰ" is about 20.35 meters long and 7.85 meters wide. There are 244 ship structure components excavated, including 3 keels, 94 shells, 63 frames, 7 frame-reinforcing parts, 11 frame-connecting plates, 3 bulkheads, 1 bulkhead-reinforcing part, 6 battens, 37 dunnage boards, 1 mast base, 1 propping rod and 17 other components.

首龙骨右侧

首龙骨反面

1 首龙骨
Stem

残长106.0cm 宽54.0cm 厚5.4cm

Length 106.0cm Width 54.0cm Thickness 5.4cm

  木材为龙脑香科龙脑香属。头部残缺。近似舌状。头部翘起，后部与主龙骨相接。首龙骨与主龙骨为直角企口搭接，首龙骨在上，主龙骨在下；在搭接处用多枚船钉按四方上下钉牢，未见补强材、铁箍、蘑菇钉。

2 主龙骨
Keel

长1425.0cm 宽45.0cm 厚15.5cm

Length 1425.0cm Width 45.0cm Thickness 15.5cm

　　木材为龙脑香科龙脑香属。基本完整。横断面为"凸"字形。主龙骨与尾龙骨为直角搭接。主龙骨与尾龙骨分别设有凹凸，定为榫、槽，主龙骨在上，为方形凹槽，尾龙骨在下，有凸榫；连接时用三根方形大木榫从上方楔入，方形大木榫上大下小，在楔入连接部位附近也钉有较大铁钉，未见铁箍。

主龙骨右侧后端局部

主龙骨反面前端局部

主龙骨反面

主龙骨右侧

3 尾龙骨
Stern

残长600.0cm 宽42.0cm 厚22.5cm
Length 600.0cm Width 42.0cm Thickness 22.5cm

木材为马鞭草科石梓属。尾部残。前部与主龙骨搭接，有与主龙骨对应的3个连接定位榫槽。

尾龙骨左侧

尾龙骨正面

尾龙骨反面

尾龙骨右侧

篇章六　船体构件
Chapter VI　Ship Structural Component

4 肋骨
Frame

肋东5

Eastern Frame No. 5

长416.5cm　宽19.0cm　厚16.7cm

Length 416.5cm　Width 19.0cm　Thickness 16.7cm

　　属船底肋骨。基本完整，两端略残。弧状。底部有两个长方形流水孔，尺寸分别为70mm×40mm、80mm×40mm。下缘有钉孔。

肋骨正面

肋骨后侧

篇章六　船体构件

Chapter VI Ship Structural Component

The Lost Pearl of Yushan ——宁波象山『小白礁Ⅰ号』出水文物精品图录

150

肋骨正面

肋骨前侧

篇章六 船体构件
Chapter VI Ship Structural Component

5 肋骨
Frame

肋东13

Eastern Frame No. 13

长362.6cm 宽21.0cm 厚17.0cm

Length 362.6cm Width 21.0cm Thickness 17.0cm

　　属船底肋骨。基本完整。中间较平整，两端起翘。底部有两个长方形流水孔，尺寸分别为60mm×35mm、90mm×30mm。下缘有钉孔。

6 肋骨
Frame

肋东16

Eastern Frame No. 16

长334.5cm 宽21.0cm 厚16.0cm

Length 334.5cm Width 21.0cm Thickness 16.0cm

  属船底肋骨。基本完整。中间较平整，一侧有一道斜削长槽，两端起翘。底部有一长方形流水孔，尺寸为80mm×40mm。下缘有钉孔。

肋骨正面

肋骨后侧

篇章六　船体构件
Chapter VI　Ship Structural Component

肋骨后侧

肋骨反面

7 肋骨
Frame

肋东21
Eastern Frame No. 21
残长199.8cm 宽17.0cm 厚17.8cm
Length 199.8cm Width 17.0cm Thickness 17.8cm

　　属船底肋骨。两端残。弧状，中部略折。底部有一个长方形流水孔，尺寸为90mm×32mm。下缘有钉孔。

肋骨前侧

肋骨反面

8 肋骨
Frame

肋东22

Eastern Frame No. 22

残长122.8cm 宽18.0cm 厚15.0cm

Length 122.8cm Width 18.0cm Thickness 15.0cm

　　属船底肋骨。两端残。中部上下削平，两端折翘。底部有一个长方形流水孔，尺寸为80mm×37mm。下缘有钉孔。

9 肋骨
Frame

肋西11

Western Frame No. 11

残长261.0cm 宽16.0cm 厚12.8cm

Length 261.0cm Width 16.0cm Thickness 12.8cm

属舷侧肋骨。两端略残。弧状。下缘有三个钉孔，尺寸分别为10mm×10mm、11mm×11mm、12mm×12mm，钉孔深度约180mm~200mm。

肋骨反面

肋骨前侧

10 隔舱板
Bulkhead

隔1
Bulkhead No. 1

残长330.3cm 厚7.0cm 高38.5cm
Length 330.3cm Width 7.0cm Height 38.5cm

　　木材为龙脑香科软坡垒属。底部较平，向两侧起弧；上部一端残，另一端开两道凹槽，应是供纵梁通过。底部设两个流水孔，尺寸为分别为74mm×42mm、80mm×45mm。隔舱板与外板以船钉钉固。

隔舱板上面

隔舱板前侧

隔舱板下面

篇章六 船体构件
Chapter VI Ship Structural Component

11 隔舱板
Bulkhead

隔2
Bulkhead No. 2

残长337.2cm 厚8.0cm 高31.5cm
Length 337.2cm Width 8.0cm Height 31.5cm

　　木材为龙脑香科龙脑香属。基本完整。底部为弧形；上部较平直，一端略残，另一端开一道凹槽。底部设一个流水孔，尺寸为92mm×48mm。隔舱板与外板以船钉钉固。

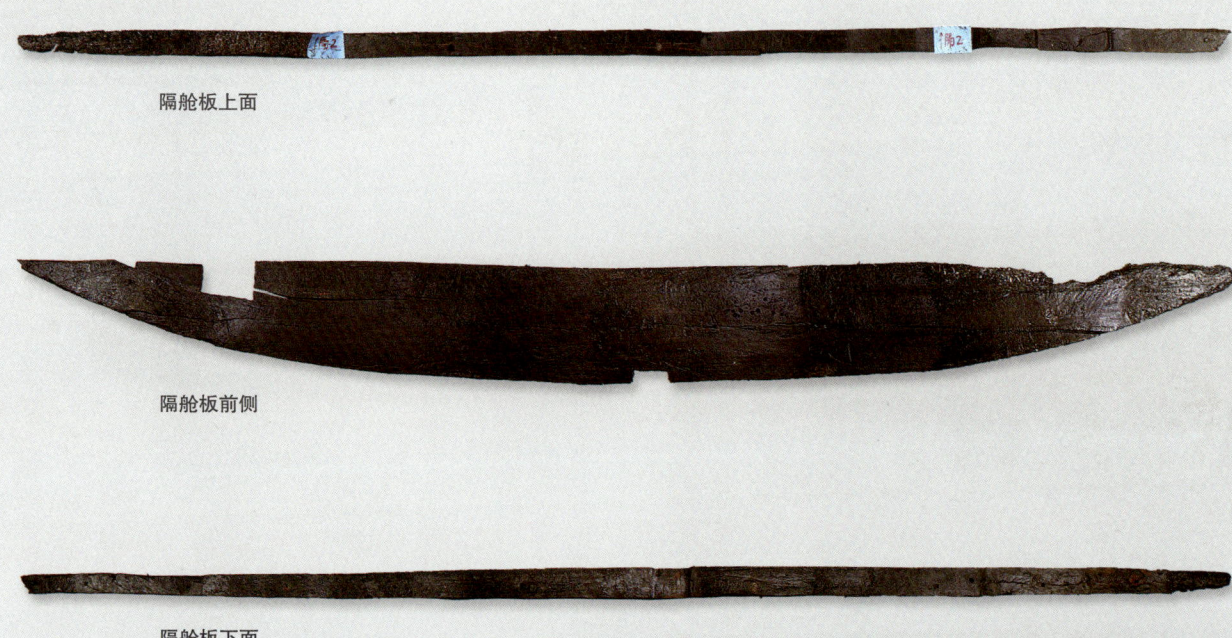

隔舱板上面

隔舱板前侧

隔舱板下面

隔舱板上面

隔舱板前侧

隔舱板下面

12 隔舱板
Bulkhead

隔3

Bulkhead No. 3

残长256.0cm 厚7.0cm 高37.8cm

Length 256.0cm　Width 7.0cm　Height 37.8cm

　　木材为龙脑香科龙脑香属。基本完整。底部为弧形；上部较平直，一端略残，另一端开一道凹槽。底部设一个流水孔，尺寸为70mm×42mm。隔舱板与外板以船钉钉固。

船壳内层板左侧

船壳内层板内面

船壳内层板外面

船壳内层板右侧

13 船壳内层板
Shell

壳东2-2/5

Eastern Shell 2-2/5

长357.2cm 宽33.2cm 厚5.0cm

Length 357.2cm Width 33.2cm Thickness 5.0cm

基本完整。边接缝为平对接，端接缝一端为平面同口，一端为滑肩同口。

14 船壳外层板
2nd Layer of Shell

壳西3-2/5

Western Shell 3-2/5

长357.0cm 宽14.0cm 厚5.0cm

Length 357.2cm Width 14.0cm Thickness 5.0cm

基本完整。边接缝为平对接，端接缝一端为平面同口。

船壳外层板左侧

船壳外层板外面

船壳外层板内面

船壳外层板右侧

篇章六　船体构件

Chapter VI　Ship Structural Component

165

铺舱板左侧

铺舱板正面

铺舱板反面

铺舱板右侧

15 铺舱板
Dunnage Board

垫3

Dunnage Board No. 3

长393.5cm 宽27.2cm 厚3.5cm

Length 393.5cm Width 27.2cm Thickness 3.5cm

木材为使君子科榄仁属。基本完整，一端开裂，一端略残。背面可辨五道肋骨印痕。

铺舱板左侧

铺舱板反面

铺舱板正面

铺舱板右侧

16 铺舱板
Dunnage Board

垫16
Dunnage Board No. 16
长136.4cm 宽26.9cm 厚2.5cm
Length 136.4cm Width 26.9cm Thickness 2.5cm

　　基本完整,两端各有一个直角口。有六个圆形孔,其中两个钉孔残存有小木桩,孔径20mm;有十二个铲钉孔。

17 铺舱板
Dunnage Board

垫27

Dunnage Board No. 27

长202.5cm 宽35.6cm 厚2.5cm

Length 202.5cm Width 35.6cm Thickness 2.5cm

　　基本完整。有十一个圆形小孔,其中四个小孔残存有小木桩,钉孔近似圆形,孔径约20mm;有两个铲钉孔。

铺舱板左侧

铺舱板正面

铺舱板反面

铺舱板右侧

18 船壳外层板
2nd Layer of Shell

壳东 7 下-3/4

Eastern Shell No.7 Bottom-3/4

长397.0cm 宽25.0cm 厚2.0cm

Length 397.0cm Width 25.0cm Thickness 2.0cm

基本完整。边接缝为平对接，端接缝一端为平面同口。

船壳外层板左侧

船壳外层板右侧

船壳外层板内面

船壳外层板外面

凸木左侧

凸木正面

凸木反面

凸木右侧

19 顶杠
Propping Rod

长125.1cm 宽22.0cm 高11.9cm

Length 125.1cm Width 22.0cm Thickness 11.9cm

　　木材为马鞭草科佩龙木属。基本完整，榫口及两端部有蛀损。顶面圆弧；两侧面与底面平直，底面开有一个长方形凹槽，尺寸为14mm×36mm；顶杠一端上部外凸40mm，另一端底部内收约140mm。该顶杠设于两道隔舱板之间，用于支撑加固舱壁结构。

桅座左侧

桅座右侧

桅座前侧

桅座后侧

桅座下面

桅座上面

20 桅座
Mast Base

长186.0cm 宽88.0cm 最厚19.0cm

Length 186.0cm Width 88.0cm Thickness 19.0cm

木材为龙脑香科软坡垒属。略残。桅座面上开有两个凹槽，槽形特殊，槽深90mm，应当为桅夹底部截面形状的写照；每个凹槽内有两个圆形孔槽，孔径20mm，当是做定位榫之用。底部平直，两侧各内收150mm、230mm。

后 记

位于浙江宁波象山石浦渔山列岛海域北渔山岛小白礁畔水下24米深处的"小白礁Ⅰ号"清代沉船遗址，于2008年首次发现，2014年完成发掘，前后历时六年之久。发掘出水后的部分文物与模拟发掘场景现正在国家水下文化遗产保护宁波基地"水下考古在中国"专题陈列中展出，船体构件同步在宁波基地沉船修复展示室内边保护边展示，相关资料与发掘报告亦已在有条不紊地整理、撰写中。为尽早向业界和社会公布水下考古成果，我们专门挑选了"小白礁Ⅰ号"1060余件出水船载文物中的部分精品和240余件出水船体构件中有代表性的构件，先期编辑成册出版，名之曰《渔山遗珠——宁波象山"小白礁Ⅰ号"出水文物精品图录》。

本图录编辑任务分工如下：器物描述：林国聪、王光远、史伟；船体构件描述：金涛、顿贺；摄影：冯毅、孙臣、李朱佳、代威巍；翻译：周昳恒、洪欣；概述、后记与全文统稿：林国聪、王结华。

中国文化遗产研究院刘曙光院长，国家文物局水下文化遗产保护中心柴晓明主任、张威书记，水下考古研究所姜波所长、办公室赵嘉斌主任，宁波市文化广电新闻出版局赵惠峰局长、舒月明副局长、徐建成处长等领导对本图录的编著给予了大力支持；宁波出版社编辑卓挺亚、王晓君等人为本图录的出版付出了辛勤劳动。值此书稿付梓之际，谨向他们致以衷心的谢意。

由于编者水平有限，本图录编著过程中出现的疏漏与错误在所难免，尚祈各位读者见谅并指正。

编者

2015年8月

Postscript

"Xiaobaijiao I" Qing Dynasty shipwreck is located in the depth of 24 meters underwater near Xiaobaijiao Reef in Yushan Archipelago in Shipu Port, Xiangshan County, Ningbo, Zhejiang Province. It was firstly discovered in 2008, and was finally excavated in 2014 with time duration of 6 years. The excavated artefacts and the site replica are displayed in the *Underwater Archaeology in China* Exhibition. Meanwhile the shipwreck components are displayed and technically preserved in the Shipwreck Conservation Area in Ningbo Base, National Center of Underwater Cultural Heritage. The related data and excavation report are in the process of editing. In order to have some of the archaeological results shown to the public as soon as possible, we have selected elaborate ones from 1060 artefacts and some typical ones from 240 ship components from "Xiaobaijiao I" shipwreck to compiled into a gallery, with the title *"Lost Pearl of Yushan—— The Boutique Atlas of 'Xiaobaijiao I ' Shipwreck in Xiangshan of Ningbo"*.

This book was compiled under the cooperation of the following staff:

Artefact Description: Lin Guocong, Wang Guangyuan, Shi Wei

Ship Structural Component Description: Jin Tao, Dun He

Photographers: Feng Yi, Sun Chen, Li Zhujia, Dai Weiwei

Translators: Zhou Yiheng, Hong Xin

Chief Editor and Chief Writer: Lin Guocong, Wang Jiehua

On the occasion of the completion of this book, we'd like to express our sincere appreciation to: Liu Shuguang, Head of Chinese Academy of Cultural Heritage; Chai Xiaoming, Director of National Center of Underwater Cultural Heritage ; Zhang Wei, Party Branch Secretary of National Center of Underwater Cultural Heritage; Jiang Bo, Director of Underwater Archaeology Department of National Center of Underwater Cultural Heritage; Zhao Jiabin, Director of the office of National Conservation Center of Underwater Cultural Heritage; Zhao Huifeng, General Director of Culture, Radio, Television, Press and Publication Bureau of Ningbo; Shu Yueming, Deputy General Director of Culture, Radio, Television, Press and Publication Bureau of Ningbo; Xu Jiancheng, Director of Cultural Relics and Museum Department of Culture, Radio, Television, Press and Publication Bureau of Ningbo and Zhuo Tingya, Wang Xiaojun, editors of Ningbo Publishing House.

Confined to the ability of the editors, there are inevitable mistakes and flaws in this atlas. Please feel free to correct us.

Editor

August, 2015

图书在版编目（CIP）数据

渔山遗珠：宁波象山"小白礁Ⅰ号"出水文物精品图录 / 宁波市文物考古研究所，象山县文物管理委员会办公室，国家文物局水下文化遗产保护中心编著. — 宁波：宁波出版社，2015.10

ISBN 978-7-5526-2255-3

Ⅰ.①渔… Ⅱ.①宁… ②象… ③国… Ⅲ.①文物—宁波市—图集 Ⅳ.① K873.553

中国版本图书馆 CIP 数据核字（2015）第 224468 号

渔山遗珠

宁波象山"小白礁Ⅰ号"出水文物精品图录

编　　著　宁波市文物考古研究所
　　　　　象山县文物管理委员会办公室
　　　　　国家文物局水下文化遗产保护中心

出版发行	宁波出版社（宁波市甬江大道1号宁波书城8号楼6楼　315040）
网　　址	http://www.nbcbs.com
责任编辑	王晓君
责任校对	王　丹
责任审读	虞姬颖
装帧设计	浙江新华图文制作有限公司
印　　刷	浙江新华数码印务有限公司
开　　本	889毫米×1194毫米　1/16
印　　张	11.75
字　　数	100千
版　　次	2015年10月第1版
印　　次	2015年10月第1次印刷
书　　号	ISBN 978-7-5526-2255-3
定　　价	268.00元

如发现缺页或倒装，影响阅读，请与承印厂联系调换。电话：0571-85155604